T0369977

Front Porches

to the

Picture Window

Randy Mink

Front Porches to the Picture Window
©2024 Randy Mink

All rights reserved. No part of this publication may be reproduced, distributed, or transmitted in any form or by any means, including photocopying, recording, or other electronic or mechanical methods, without the prior written permission of the publisher, except in the case of brief quotations embodied in critical reviews and certain other non-commercial uses permitted by copyright law.

Contents

Introduction

As a writer, my job is to make you, the reader, feel something. To make you want to go from one chapter to the next. To stir up an emotion within you, a sentiment, or bring back a memory, good or bad, and allow you to become part of the story. My goal is to make you feel happy and sad, glad and mad, and all the emotions in between. To allow you to feel what I'm feeling as a writer. If I can do that, I've done my job as a writer.

This book may be unlike any you have ever read. It has been a lifetime in the making—my lifetime. It's changed and evolved many times through the years. I will break all the rules as a writer and let you get to know the real me, not hidden in a character or a plot; although I am a character and there are plots, it will be an open book between you, the reader, and me, the writer.

I may break some grammatical rules. There may be commas where they shouldn't be, but there are no commas where they should be. I may go crazy and even end a sentence with a preposition. But what I will do in this book is follow Ernest Hemingway's two greatest rules of writing. Write the simplest and truest sentence I know, and write what I know with honesty people aren't used to anymore.

If I had to describe this book, I would describe it as an autobiographical anthology. It's written in four distinct sections through four distinct periods of my life. Each section had been planned to be its own individual book once upon a time during different periods of my life. Many of these stories are old, and a few are new. You may even detect a slight difference in my writing style through the book's different sections as my style has evolved, like me, into the person and writer I am today.

I grew up a baby boomer in rural southwest Ohio and the hills of southeast Kentucky before moving to Florida at age sixteen. Long before the internet, cell phones, and all the distractions of the current world. It was a simpler time, and my best memories are of listening to my parents, relatives, and friends sitting on the porch or in the yard under a tree in the fall of the night, telling stories. That's where I developed a love of storytelling. You'll have to read the whole book to understand the picture window.

So this book is all about stories from my life: the good and the bad. I hope I've written it well enough to make you laugh and to make you cry, but most of all, to make you think. I pray that when you get to the end, you will say, "I hated for this book to end." If I've intrigued you enough, pull up a chair, relax, forget about your problems, and join me as we journey through my life, from the Front Porches to the Picture Window.

Section One

Front Porches:
Where the Sidewalks End
and the
Dirt Paths Begin

Grandma Mink, Dad, and Mom holding me, Grove Street, Maud,
Ohio, 1959

Chapter 1
Maud—Where Life Began

Crossroads Grocery (ca 1960s, photo courtesy of Tim Reese)

I'm southern, having lived most of my life in the cracker country of south-central Florida. It's the natural Florida of cattle, orange groves, and phosphate mines. Not the tourist Florida of beaches and amusement parks as seen in TV advertisements. I'm a Kentuckian by heritage, but I was born in Hamilton, Ohio. After my birth, my parents took me home to the little white house with black trim and a small detached garage with an outhouse behind it, located on the curve of Grove Street and Third Street in Maud, Ohio. This home is the place of my earliest and some of my fondest memories.

I have yet to learn about the beginning of Maud as a community. It's an unincorporated area in what's called West Chester nowadays. When I was born, it consisted of less than a dozen streets lined with many other tiny frame houses just like ours sitting close together. To most of the people in the surrounding communities, Maud was just a hamlet full of poor, ignorant hillbillies who had moved north after World War II and the Korean War to escape the hard life and poverty of southeast Kentucky. They found work in factories around Cincinnati that paid better wages and offered an easier life than farming the rocks and red clay on the hillsides back home in Kentucky. They worked in factories like Proctor and Gamble, General Electric, all the car manufacturing plants, or Stearns and Foster in Lockland, where most of my uncles and my dad worked.

Perhaps in our old age, our fondest memories of our youth are due to our childhood innocence. I prefer to keep it that way. Growing up in the 1960s, Maud had its share of problems, but from my perspective, my family protected me from them, and I was allowed to be a kid. My earliest childhood memory was sitting in a high chair in that little kitchen; I'm not sure what age was, but I was small enough to have the neighbor's child, Timmy Stevens, sitting with me.

Timmy's dad, Claiborne, worked driving trucks with my dad. His mother, Yvonne, the first crush I remember having, was my mother's friend. While our parents sat talking and drinking coffee, somehow Timmy and I reached the salt and pepper shakers and unscrewed the lids off. No one noticed as we smiled at each other, dumping the pepper all over the high-chair tray until we got it in our eyes and both started screaming from the burning pain. I remembered that pain years later when I was pepper sprayed in the face by a policeman. And I remembered it once again, when I was a mayor in Bowling Green, Florida. While riding with a police officer, on the right side of the law this time, I accidently sprayed myself in the face with pepper spray. Always check which direction the wind is blowing from and the nozzle is facing; if not, pain is always a great teacher.

Eating a whole bowl of butter is a great teacher too. Well, not that great, but it will make you vomit. At about three years old and constantly curious and adventurous, I wandered into the garage behind the house. I was good at getting lids off things, especially pepper shakers and gas cans. I got the cap off my dad's metal gas can in the garage. I bent my head down and took a few whiffs of gas. It smelled good to me, so I took a few more whiffs. I put the cap back on and staggered back into the house.

My mom smelled gas all over me and freaked out. She thought I had been in the garage drinking the gas and called the doctor. I didn't understand her concern. I might have looked like I was a high three-year-old from the gas fumes (which might explain the loss of a few brain cells and my drug use later in the 1970s), but I wasn't stupid; I knew not to drink gas. The doctor assured my mom on the phone that I probably hadn't drunk any gas, but he suggested feeding me butter until I puked to make sure. I sat there at that same table where the pepper incident happened, buzzing a little from the gateway drug of gas fumes, eating a whole container of butter until I puked. My mother then inspected my vomit, as only a loving mother could, and saw that all in my stomach was melted butter and some oatmeal. Surprisingly, I love butter and pepper today, but only as condiments, not the main course. And I still really enjoy the smell of gas. Occasionally, I'll even take a whiff or two while pumping gas. But oatmeal, I still don't care much for it.

By the time I was four years old, the outhouse was gone, and we had indoor plumbing, thanks to some of the hoodlums in the neighborhood. One Halloween, some teenagers decided to go around and tip over all the outhouses in Maud. It was the hot topic of conversation for weeks in Maud – everyone kept guessing who had done it. The list of suspects would change every time I overheard the grown-ups talking about it. Sometimes it must have the Phelps boys, sometimes the Shepherd boys, and other times the Bussell or Horton boys. I've always thought some Minks may have been the perpetrators, namely my oldest brother, Gary, and a couple of first cousins,

Bill and Greg. Whoever did it probably wouldn't have toppled their toilet; well, except my brother Gary probably would have. It should have been a pretty straightforward case to solve.

My dad and Claiborne hid in the garage with a pistol for several nights after the crime spree in case they returned to the crime scene to upright the outhouses. That was their story to my mom and Yvonne anyway. Mostly, they just wanted to sit outside, drink beer, and swap stories and took the pistol along as a ruse to convince their wives they were hot on the trail of the toilet tippers. No one ever confessed or was caught; by Christmas time, it was all but forgotten. Still, I wonder all these many years later if some rookie detective will come sneaking around to match DNA found on a gas cap left at the scene.

My paternal grandma, Cordie Mink, lived three houses from us on Third Street. She may have been the last resident of Maud to get an inside bathroom because her outhouse didn't get toppled over. When I graduated from high school in Florida in 1977, I hitchhiked from Florida to Maud. I planned to take a year off from school, hitchhike around the country to gather stories, go to college and get a journalism degree, become a writer, and write about my adventures traveling around the country. It didn't quite work out that way, but I made it to Grandma's with a few change of clothes and a kilo of marijuana. That's how I can remember she still had an outhouse in 1977. I would go out several times a day and smoke pot in it while I was staying with her during that time.

One day, I came in through the backdoor, all red-eyed and happy after about my fourth or fifth trip to the outhouse, and there was Grandma standing in her kitchen, her hand on her hips, giving me the stare down.

"What's the matter, Grandma?" I asked.

"I know what you've been doing and why you go out there so much."

Oh crap! I thought. The gig is up. She has gone through my bag and found my pot. The one fortunate thing I thought of was that she couldn't flush it down the toilet because there wasn't one in the house.

I asked, "Why's that, Grandma?"

"You're going out there playing with yourself," she said.

You could have pushed me over with a feather. If I had a list of a thousand things my grandma could have said, that would not have been on the list. It took me a few seconds to realize if my stoned ears heard what I thought they heard. And now, my little stoned brain had to make a decision. Do I let my grandma think her grandson is a pothead or a pervert? I thought for a minute and remembered my older brothers, Gary and Terry, had lived with Grandma when they were teenagers, so I chose the obvious choice.

"You got me, Grandma. Ain't no one can pull anything over on you," I answered, busting out laughing so hard I couldn't breathe.

"But you're a Mink, just like your brothers, your daddy, and your grandpa, so I should have known."

By then, I had to sit down. I had tears streaming down my face, and my stomach was cramping. I was laughing hard. The buzz from being stoned only made it worse. Grandma started laughing and sat down too. My laughing was making her laugh. Finally, after we had regained our composure, Grandma asked if I'd like some hoe bread. That started another round of laughter, but eventually, we sat there eating hoe bread; she put blackberry jam on hers, and I put maple syrup on mine.

Grandma Mink was one-fourth Cherokee but looked full-blooded. I'm unsure if it was a Kentucky thing or a Cherokee thing or both. But, ever since I could remember, she always had hoe bread sitting on a plate, either on the table or on the stove. If you are wondering what hoe bread is, it's as if fried corn bread and a pancake had a love child. That's hoe bread, and Grandma made the best.

During that visit, Grandma and I sat at her kitchen table and talked for hours every day and night. She told me details about her life that I could never imagine growing up. She explained how her stepfamily had abandoned her. When you're young and look at older people, it's hard to picture their lives when they were young. She was a child when her father died and her mother remarried. Her stepfamily didn't want her, and she was forced to move in and be raised by her older siblings. When her mother died, she was forbidden to attend her mother's funeral by her stepfather. She spoke of stories of abuse and betrayal. All those years later, she still felt the pain and grief from her childhood.

Grandma told me all the details of my grandpa, who had died before I was born. She told me of the shootout with the county constables in Kentucky, a story I'd heard throughout my youth from my dad and aunts, who were present but were children at the time. I've read the newspaper clippings and a chapter dedicated to the event in a book, *The Harper's of Pongo Ridge*, by Christine McKinney, but none had the insight that Grandma had. She was the only surviving adult present during the shootout and knew the whole back-story behind it. The deputies kicked in the door, without warning or a warrant, looking for my grandpa and his moonshine. Grandma tried to block them and positioned herself between the deputies and her five children. One constable slammed her against the wall, opening a cut in her forehead, while screaming at her to divulge my grandpa's location and the location of the still. She wouldn't say a word, which only infuriated them more.

One of my aunts snuck out and ran to fetch my grandpa, who was plowing with a mule in the backfield. The constables had left the house and were out in front when grandpa slipped in the back. He saw my grandma bleeding and crying and grabbed his pump shotgun off the wall. He loaded the only three rounds of birdshot into the gun and mumbled, "Reckon this is all I need."

Grandma said by the front door was a picture of Jesus praying in the garden of Gethsemane. Grandpa looked up at the picture, racked a round in the chamber, and said, "Well, Lord, looks like it's just you and me." Then he threw open the front door to confront the constables. The constables immediately began shooting, riddling the house with bullets. Grandpa shot the first constable, which peeled a portion of his scalp from the top of his head. Grandma said as the shots were hitting the house, she had the kids huddling behind an overturned table. Then she realized the oldest, my aunt Rosie, who was fourteen at the time, was missing. Grandma had to crawl over and pull my aunt Rosie from the front window, where she had stuck her head out and was cussing the constables and yelling at my grandpa: "Kill every damn one of 'em, Pops, kill every damn one of 'em." At this point, my grandma saw my grandpa go down on one knee and thought he had been wounded badly. Grandpa had been shot in his left forearm. Unable to rack the second round into the shotgun with his wounded arm, he had dropped to his knee to use the ground as leverage against the butt of the gun to rack the round with his one good arm.

He then shot the second constable in the stomach. Seeing both constables on the ground, the third constable, the ring leader, took off running toward the barn for cover, firing wildly over his shoulder. Grandpa used the ground again to rack his third and final round, into the shotgun. Just as the third constable was about to turn the corner of the barn, Grandpa fired, hitting him squarely in the backside, and down he went. Out of ammunition now, and fearing there may be more, Grandpa ran next door to his brother's home to get more shotgun shells.

The constables were only wounded with the birdshot. While Grandpa was at his brother's, the three constables got up and ran for their lives. When the ring leader arrived in the town of Livingston, about eight miles from my grandpa's farm, he looked like a wildcat had gotten a hold of him. His cuts and scrapes from running through the briars and brambles, thinking Grandpa was on his trail to finish him off, were far worse than the many pellets the doctor removed from his derriere. Grandpa removed the bullet from his arm and turned himself in to the sheriff. He was arrested and released until the trial.

Grandma told me about the trial, and I have been told the same story by many who were also in court that day. In the end, the judge asked my grandpa to stand and asked if he had anything to say before pronouncing his sentence. Grandpa rose from his chair with his arm in a sling from his wound and said, "Yes sir, Your Honor, I do," and turned directly to look at the constables, still bandaged up from their wounds. "If I'd known those son of bitches weren't dead when I went to get more ammunition, I would have dragged their sorry asses to my chopping block, taken my ax, and cut their damn heads off."

The courtroom erupted in laughs and cheers. The constables had considered themselves above the law and had been running moonshine themselves. They were trying to eliminate the competition by trying to put my grandpa out of the business. Folks liked Grandpa's "shine" better. The judge regained order in the courtroom and said to my grandpa, "Harve, I've known you for a long time, and I have no doubts that you would have done exactly that. I fine you ten dollars for disturbing the peace."

The judge then turned his wrath on the constables, who had been abusing their authority for quite some time toward the citizens of that area through intimidation and bullying. He then advised them that if they should ever meet my grandpa on the street in Mt. Vernon, it would be in their best interest to cross to the other side; they may not be as lucky next time. According to Grandma, the judge and Grandpa were good friends, and he was one of Grandpa's best customers. Grandpa quickly got his ten dollars back in moonshine sales to the judge. It was Kentucky hill justice at its finest.

I never did finish hitchhiking around the country as I had intended. However, during those weeks I stayed with my grandma in Maud, I was given more stories and learned more than I ever would have otherwise. I learned stories of my people and my heritage.

I returned to Florida after staying with Grandma and got into trouble myself. It broke my heart when I realized, while hiding in the mountains of North Carolina, that federal agents had entered and searched her home with warrants for my arrest. It gave her flashbacks to the 1930s and my grandpa in the hills of Kentucky, and I was not too fond of the fact that I was responsible for that. But just like with my grandpa, she wouldn't say a word about my whereabouts. During those weeks staying with my Grandma, I realized that Grandma during her lifetime, just like her Cherokee ancestors before her, had walked her own "trail of tears."

Around Maud, my grandma was an icon. Everyone knew her as Ma Mink, or Grandma, and everyone loved her. She lived her Christian virtues. If you were thirsty, she'd give you something to drink. If you were hungry, she'd feed you. If you needed a place to stay, she'd put you up. I often walked her to Crossroads to buy her a plug of Days Work chewing tobacco. She'd come home, sit in her rocking chair, chew her tobacco, and read the Bible for hours. And if you went to the outhouse too often, she'd call you out on it.

It was the perfect childhood growing up in Maud in the 1960s. Family surrounded me. We all lived in Maud, my mom and dad, two older brothers, all four of Dad's sisters, and their families, including fifteen first cousins and Grandma. You didn't have to be born in southeast Kentucky to pick up the slang and accent; you just had to be raised in Maud. When I was about four and a half, we moved out of Maud into the country on Hamilton-Mason Road, about a mile north. But we were always visiting Maud, and Maud always felt like home.

At the town's main intersection was the Crossroads store with a barber shop beside it and Bob Tate's service station across the street. I always looked for soda pop bottles to take to Crossroads to get the three-cent deposit back on the bottles to exchange for penny candy. Back then, service stations were all full-service. Dad would get his gas at Bob Tate's, and while Bob was washing the windshield or checking the oil, he and Dad would discuss all the world's problems, like hoodlums tipping over outhouses.

Bob Tate left a lasting impression on me. Although all I can remember of him are his crew-cut hair and a red grease rag hanging out of his back pocket, I named my first cat after him. Bobbie Dewey Mae Mink Bob Tate Mink. Truthfully, it was named after three people but it included Bob Tate. It was a yellow and white tuxedo that liked to eat mayonnaise, or that was Dad's explanation when I found it with a mayonnaise jar stuck on its head. I was crying, thinking the cat would suffocate. I cried even more when my dad held the cat as our neighbor Claiborne smashed the mayonnaise jar with a claw hammer to free the cat. Dad assured me the cat would be alright; he only used up one of his nine lives, but he still had eight. I've had several yellow and white tuxedo cats throughout my life. I have named them all the same. Even as I write this, I have Bobby Dewey Mae Mink Bob Tate Mink the eighth or ninth—I've lost count—lying beside my writing desk. Bob Tate has long since passed, but as long as I have a yellow and white cat, he will always be immortalized.

My youngest brother, Ron, had not yet been born, so I was the youngest of the Mink clan in Maud. It had its perks; I didn't have to worry about many hoodlums bullying me because I had two older brothers and fifteen first cousins to protect me. It had its downside too. My cousins were more like older siblings and had the same rights to clobber and torment me as my brothers. You'll read more about that later in the chapter titled "Club Initiations."

There was no internet, gaming, or entertainment, and being the youngest, I sometimes was the entertainment. Countless times I was held by my ankles over the hole in my aunt Rosie's outhouse until I would say "Uncle" or whatever the word of the day was. I remember playing hide-and-seek and hiding in bushes while one cousin pretended to count to a thousand. They would all sneak off and leave me alone in the dark until I would run from my hiding spot and tag home base and holler "Safe," thinking I'd won, only to realize they had all snuck away and I was the only one left playing. Nowadays, some would think that's cruel, but I wouldn't have had my childhood any other way.

My cousin Debbie was only a year older than me. We both had reddish hair and freckles and rode our bikes around Maud, telling everyone we were twins. Sometimes, when we would swing by our Aunt Rosie's on Fourth Street, she would dress herself up as a witch and holler at us from the front door, "I'm going to get you and your little dog too!" I didn't understand her saying that; I didn't have a dog then, just a cat that kept getting a mayonnaise jar stuck on its head. But it was still scary, even if we knew it was Aunt Rosie in disguise, especially after you had watched *The Wizard of Oz* the night before. It made us peddle faster up the street to Debbie's mom, my aunt Rene. My aunt Rene and I shared the same birthday. I was her pick of the litter. No matter when I would stop to see her, even years later, she always had a piece of cake or pie stuck back for me.

One Halloween, when we were four or five years old, we went trick-or-treating. Maud was the best place in the world to trick-or-treat. There were many houses close together, and almost everyone gave out lots of candy. I had a character plastic mask of Mighty Mouse with a rubber band that stretched around my head and held the Halloween mask tight against my face. My rubber band broke, so I had to walk around holding it up against my face with one hand and my candy bag with the other. I must have been dragging my candy bag on the street, and it had worn a hole in the bottom. When we returned to my aunt Rene's to see how much loot we had collected, most of my candy had unknowingly fallen out of my bag behind me. I was heartbroken. Without thinking twice, my cousin Debbie gave me half of her candy.

Cousins were indeed like siblings growing up in my family. They might hold you by your ankles over the toilet until you said "Uncle" or put you in a headlock and give you "noogies" on the top of your head, but if a big bully gave you trouble, they were the first to join the fight, and if you lost all your Halloween candy, they were the first to share theirs.

On Halloween of 1968, we lived in a rural area a mile outside Maud. My youngest brother, Ron, was now four years old, and my oldest brother, Gary, was away in Vietnam, serving in the Marine Corps. Ron and I were begging Mom to take us trick-or-treating in Maud, but the weather was terrible, and she didn't want to go. We tormented her until she threatened us with a whipping. Finally, she relented that we could go, but only if our older brother, Terry, would take us, and he had to stay with us.

My little brother, Ron, and I went into the living room where our brother Terry, who was sixteen years old and had a car and a driver's license, was sitting on the couch watching TV and biting his fingernails. It wasn't until now that I noticed a big circle of mud around my baby brother's mouth.

"You been eating dirt again?"

He nodded his head happily with a big smile. I was curious to know why he ate dirt; maybe he was mineral deficient or was just a little strange, but he loved the stuff. He reminded me of the little boy, Leon, on the Andy Griffith show, who was always eating a peanut-butter-and-jelly sandwich that left a giant ring around his mouth, but instead of peanut butter and jelly, my brother had a big circle of mud around his.

"Mom said we could go trick-or-treating in Maud if you would take us, but you had to stay with us," I told Terry.

"No way, Jose." For some reason, this had become his favorite saying, and still, to this day, I don't know why.

"Come on, Terry; it's Halloween. We'll give you some of our candy." I knew Terry had a terrible sweet tooth.

"I'll make you a deal. I get half of the candy, and you have to cash in all your pop bottles at Crossroads and give me the money for gas."

"No way! I've been picking them up for three weeks and have almost five dollars' worth. I'll give you half my pop bottles, and *you* have to take them to Crossroads. You get a fourth of our candy, and mud mouth here has to wash his face."

Ron had been moving his head back and forth with a big smile following the negotiations between Terry and me until I mentioned washing his face; then, he frowned and punched me in the arm and said, "No way, Jose." I hated that saying. Not him too, I thought.

I punched him back and said, "You want some candy, don't you? No one will want to give you candy looking like that. You look like you've been sucking a hog."

Terry was sitting there thinking of a counteroffer, but I could tell the candy and gas money were enticing him, and we were close to an agreement.

"Okay, here's my final offer. I'll take half the pop bottles, and you take an extra bag and ask for candy to send to your brother in Vietnam. I get that bag, and you two keep your candy. Deal?"

My brother Terry had just put my nine-year-old conscious in a moral dilemma. I weighed my options carefully. Lose half my pop bottle fortune, and tell a very wrong lie that, if found out, would get me beat half to death, but I would get candy. Or I would keep my pop bottles, not go trick-or-treating, and not get candy. The answer was obvious; I looked at Terry and said, "Deal!" I looked at Ron, smiling and nodding his muddy mouth yes.

While Mom dragged my baby brother into the bathroom and washed his face, Terry and I made homemade costumes and grabbed three bags. We all jumped in Terry's car, and off we went to Maud with visions of candy dancing in our heads.

It was windy, cold, and drizzling rain, but it worked to the advantage of those of us that were hardcore trick-or-treaters. A lot of mothers had kept their children home because of the weather. I figured those poor kids didn't have a sixteen-year-old brother with a driver's license, a car, and a sweet tooth like our brother's. It was going to be a good night of trick-or-treating. I could feel it.

The residents of Maud, generous by nature, were more than willing to fill our bags, especially the bag designated for my brother in Vietnam. Not only were they charitable, but they were also very patriotic. Most parents in Maud either had a son or had a friend or neighbor who had a son who had been to Vietnam, or was already in Vietnam, or was waiting to go to Vietnam, and most knew my big brother, Gary, was there.

But then it happened. When I would ask at every house, "Can I have an extra piece of candy for my brother in Vietnam?" the guilt would weigh me down. Not only was telling this awful lie to get the extra candy getting to me, but I was getting pretty slighted on the candy end of the deal too. My little brother, Ron, somewhere along the way, had grabbed up another handful of dirt and stuck it in his mouth. The mud, combined with the drool from the green tootsie pop he'd snuck out of his bag and had been sucking on, made him look like he had green gills. He looked like *The Creature from the Black Lagoon* had a baby, tied a diaper around his neck for a cape, and sent him out of the swamp to find candy. But it was working for him. He was loading up on the candy.

Folks would say, "Ahhh, aren't you cute! What are you supposed to be, little boy?"

I would turn him around and show them the big, squiggly "S" from the failed attempt at a Superman emblem Terry had drawn on a big white diaper with a magic marker and tied around his neck like a cape.

I would reply, "He's supposed to be Superman," when I wanted to answer. "He's a dirt-eating baby gill man, and me and the guy sitting in the car smoking cigarettes are big, fat liars, here to con you out of extra candy." But then I would ask, "Can I have an extra piece for my brother in Vietnam?" They would throw a heaping handful in the Vietnam bag, give gill boy another handful because he was so stinking cute, and I would get just three or four pieces, and on and on it went, all evening.

Finally, the charade was over, and we headed home with a bountiful loot of candy. It was the largest haul in the history of trick-or-treating. The ride was silent except for the rustling of candy papers in the backseat, where little Superman was adding color to his gills by opening and sucking on a red tootsie pop. Terry and I were feeling the guilt of our deceit; we certainly weren't acting like we had hit the mother lode of candy.

We entered the living room and put the candy on the couch. Terry and I sat on the couch and stared at the TV. As fate would have it, the evening news with Walter Cronkite was on the channel. He was doing his nightly report on the Vietnam War. We watched as he told of the American deaths that day and showed footage of muddy marines and soldiers walking through rice paddies. Then footage of the bloodied and wounded being loaded by their buddies onto medivac helicopters. All I could think of was my brother over there, and I could see, by the look on Terry's face, he was thinking the same thing.

Mom entered the room, took one look at Ron, snatched him by his cape, and dragged him kicking and screaming down the hall to wash his face again, hollering at him the whole way about his dirt-eating addiction. That's when Terry and I decided on a whole new deal. We would send the Vietnam bag to Gary in the next care package mailed. We would let "little cutie" keep his candy minus three handfuls, two for Gary's bag and one for mine. Terry and I would split my bag. Terry started thinking that he too would probably be drafted and sent to Vietnam in a couple of years. He told me I could keep my pop bottles.

"You think Ronald will notice we took some of his candy?" Terry asked.

"Naw, I'll give him some extra tootsie pops and dirt tomorrow."

Growing up in Maud in the 1960s, it was Americana at its best. No, it wasn't perfect; no place ever is, but as a child protected from the world and surrounded by family and love, it was perfect for me. I mentioned early in this story that the residents may have been looked down upon as ignorant hillbillies by the elite of Cincinnati, but they were far more than that. Yes, some, like my dad, may have lacked formal education, but they had things that nobody could teach. Things that could only be learned in those hills and hollers, growing up in Appalachia during the Great Depression. Things like faith, hard work, loyalty, honesty, integrity, never giving up, and, most of all, your word is your word, and it's sacred. And this they taught to their children.

They fought in wars, came home, moved north, and poured out their sweat working in the factories and steel mills to pursue a better life and education for their families, which they hadn't been afforded. They may have left the hills, but the mountains of Appalachia never left them. They took those values learned, and they did exactly what they set out to do; they gave their families an opportunity for a better life and education. Ignorant hillbillies? There's no such thing. That's just Hollywood making money by creating stereotypes. They were visionaries, and they passed those visions onto their children. When those visions came to pass, many retired and returned to those hills and hollers to live out their lives, satisfied with their choices. Those people of Maud from that era were and always will be my people.

Epilogue

In March 2020, Vietnam finally killed my oldest brother, Gary. He died of brain cancer from exposure to Agent Orange during the war. A few months later, on July 5th, which, ironically, was Gary's birthday, my brother Terry died in his sleep from a heart attack. Terry never got drafted; he joined the navy before his number was called and spent the remainder of the war aboard the aircraft carrier *USS John F. Kennedy*.

My brother Ron, and his late wife, Carla, drove from Florida and met me at my home in Kentucky, and from there, we drove to Terry's funeral in West Chester, Ohio, near Maud. Neither of us had been in the area in years. After the funeral, we drove around where we had once lived outside Maud. What had once been farmland and dairies were now houses stacked upon houses for as far as the eye could see. Most of everything was unrecognizable.

When we came to Maud, Bob Tate's gas station and Crossroads store had long been gone and replaced by other businesses and mini strip malls. It was sad to see those landmarks gone. However, I was encouraged when I turned onto Third Street, where my grandma had lived. The interior of Maud looked much the way it had in my youth. It was like a memory oasis in a desert of subdivisions.

We drove around every street in Maud, pointing out all the locations where our relatives had resided. I only have one first cousin, JoAnn, who still lives in Maud. I stopped in front of the house where I was born. I could still see the garage in the back of our tiny house, where I had sniffed the gas can and had to eat butter. I could almost point to the spot where Claybourne Stevens had busted the jar off my cat's head.

It was an emotional day. An old saying says you can never go home, but that's only partially true. Some consider home a place, but a home is never a place. Home is a feeling. Home is the family, friends, and those you love who share that location. The location of a home can change throughout a lifetime. But the feeling of home never will. Home is where love and peace are an ever-present memory. Maud is a place that was once my home. But Maud will always be where my home began.

Chapter 2

Initiations into the Brothers' and Cousins' Club

We moved from Maud when I was almost five years old. We only moved a mile and a half north of Maud into a rural area onto Hamilton-Mason Road. We had a barn and a pond, along with horses, chickens, hogs, and all my dad's coon dogs. My only playmates during this time were my two oldest brothers, Gary and Terry, along with a couple of cousins on my mom's side that lived next door, Gene Harris and Lonnie Lisle. My little brother, Ron, was born soon after we moved there.

My older brothers and cousins were all in their teens, and the only way they would allow me to hang around with them was if I joined their clubs. To be a member of their club meant you had to pass the club's initiation. The funny thing about these clubs was that as soon as I passed the initiation, the club would be disbanded, and they'd form a new club. Of course, with each new club came a new initiation, usually more challenging than the last. Whenever I asked why they didn't have to pass the initiations, I was told they had already passed them when they joined. No one outside the clubs ever witnessed this. It was possible but doubtful. Whenever I would fail on my first few attempts, they would encourage me to keep trying because, as they would say, "It took Lonnie and Terry a couple of tries to pass their first time too." Never giving up always served to help me to overcome defeat later in life through perseverance because I always remembered, if those two knot heads can do it, I can too.

Looking back, these clubs had some of the most significant influences on my life, the things I enjoy, and the lessons I've learned. Passing the initiations helped lead me to do the things I've done in my life: the good and the stupid.

I can't remember all the clubs. The trauma may have blocked some of them from my psyche. Here's a list of some clubs I was allowed to join after passing the initiations.

The "**Swing Across the Fifty-Foot-Deep Gully on a Grapevine Club.**" This might have been my favorite because this was the only initiation I got to do before anyone else. Later, my dad told me they let me go first to make sure the grapevine wasn't going to break when they swung me out. I don't think my loving brothers and cousins would do such a thing. Still, thinking back now, since I was so much smaller than them then, it would explain why they attached a concrete block to me before they pushed me out of the tree and over the gully. This club is why I enjoy zip-lining like I do, or riding the alpine coaster in Pigeon Forge, and why I have never been afraid of heights.

The "**Suspended in Mid-air in the Barn with Two Ropes Attached to My Belt Loops on Both Sides of My Britches and Spun Head Over Heels Until I Puked or the Belt Loops Broke Club.**" I'm sure this is where I get my love for amusement park rides. Being woozy or dizzy has always seemed like a part of life. There was also a variation of this club, if I didn't puke or my belt loops didn't break, called the "suspended in midair in a barn with two ropes attached to my belt while being soaked down with pond water and somebody throwing dried horse manure on me with a shovel club." I'm not sure what life lesson this influenced other than that I now surely love the smell of horse manure in the mornings.

Then there was my cousin Lonnie's favorite club, the "**Peeing on an Electric Fence Club.**" Lonnie must have liked this club because he would often join me in this initiation even though he was already in the club. The "peeing on an electric fence club" was usually disbanded and reformed every time my dad would stretch a new electric fence for the horses. Cousin Lonnie was a little strange like that.

I have to admit this club prepared me for when I fell in love with Annette Funicello from the old Mickey Mouse Club TV show in the 1960s. Whenever Annette appeared on the show, I would wet my lips, run across the room, and kiss that old black-and-white, tube-type television square in her mouth. Those old tube-type TVs needed to be grounded better. They built up a tremendous amount of static electricity on the picture tube. When my big, juicy lips would touch Annette's big, juicy lips on the TV screen, the sparks would fly, and that static electric charge would pop and send me reeling backward across the living room. It didn't deter me; I'd fly across that living room every day and learn there's a fine line between true love and electrocution. Then came the day she broke my heart, and I was devastated. I saw Annette kiss Frankie Avalon in a movie called *Beach Blanket Bingo*.

This club and kissing the TV taught me many things that have stayed with me throughout my life. Although sometimes in life, things may look harmless, looks can be deceiving, and they can hurt you and break your heart. I learned that electricity, women, and love should all be treated with respect and care. If not, you can expect to feel pain, either radiating up your groin throughout your body or flying across a living room floor. Or, the worst pain of all, feeling heartbroken when your love kisses and plays Beach Blanket Bingo with a Frankie Avalon.

Also, I learned my cousin Lonnie was a little weird, and still, to this day, I will not go anywhere with my cousin Lonnie if there's an electric fence anywhere in the area.

Last but not least was the club that ended all the club joining and initiations with my brothers and cousins. Like I said earlier, portions of some of the other initiations have been blocked from my psyche, but I remember this one vividly. The most famous club of all, the "**Standing by the Road Naked and Waving at Five Cars Club**." It had the most significant influence out of all the clubs in my life and explains why I hate wearing clothes but love to wave at cars. Later in life, this earned me the nickname "Commando Rando." I also contribute this club to the many skin cancers I've had to have cut out and burnt off during my later life.

The initiation consisted of me standing butt-naked next to the road in front of our home. It sounds pretty easy, except we lived out in the country at the time surrounded by farms. There was very little traffic. And it was August, and hot, and a very sunny day. I got sunburned so bad I blistered all over. And I mean all over. Even today, when the dermatologist checks me for skin cancer and says, "Well, I probably don't need to check you down there," I roll my eyes and say, "Yes, you might; you don't know my story."

That first hour only one car came by. I stood naked in the ditch line and waved. The car slowed, the driver honked their horn, laughed, and waved back. The second-hour traffic seemed to pick up. Two cars passed with the same results: a honk, a laugh, and a wave. Then a farmer on a tractor passed. He just stared as he drove slowly by with a confused look and hesitantly gave me a nod. My brothers yelled from behind the bushes, where they were hiding, "Tractors don't count!"

I was thirsty, and my skin was beginning to burn. I forgot all that and started to feel hopeful as I heard what sounded like a truck topping the hill and heading toward me. It was a truck, my dad's truck. As my dad drove by, I just smiled and waved at him, and he returned the wave right before he locked up his brakes and came to a screeching halt right next to me.

He didn't ever turn in the drive. He just parked right there on Hamilton-Mason Road and got out of the truck with it still running. He walked around the front of the truck toward me and said, "Son, what in Sam-hell are you doing standing out here by the road naked waving at cars?"

"I'm joining a club, Dad. I have to wave at five cars, and you're number four. Only one more to go," I said proudly.

"Where are your brothers and your mother at?" Dad asked.

"Gary and Terry were in the bushes helping me count cars until they saw you; then they ran off somewhere. Mom is tending to Ronald and watching *As the World Turns* I think."

"Alright, well . . ."

I could tell Dad was mad by the way he was shaking his head and cussing to himself. But I think he felt a little sorry for me. He said, "You better get your naked self in that house right now before another car comes by. Get yourself a cold bath on that burn and some clothes on. If I see you doing this again, I'll jerk a knot in your hind end and blister your behind."

I'm sure he could have jerked a knot in my hind end, but I doubt he could have blistered my butt worse than the sun already had. From the sounds my two older brothers made when Dad caught up with them, I'm pretty sure they had wished the sun had blistered their behinds instead of Dad. Dad initiated them into his exclusive "**I can't sit down for a week club.**" After that, all the clubs were disbanded. I had to stay in the house out of the sun for the next few days. I'm not sure what hurt worse, watching *Days of Our Lives* and *As the World Turns* or the sunburn. I never stood by a road naked and waved at cars again until the mid-1970s, when streaking was all the rage. Those early days had taught me a lesson. I did it at night so that I wouldn't get sunburned.

Today, it's sad many kids grow up in small families, and families have spread far apart across the country. And if they have cousins, they're not raised with them like I was. I had three brothers, fifteen first cousins on my dad's side of the family, and fourteen on my mom's side. I had the best and most fun childhood anyone could ever imagine. Some might read this and think, "Oh my gosh, those initiations were terrible things." No, they weren't; those things taught me never to be afraid to try. I learned to face my fears and never give up. I knew my family had my back. They loved me and wouldn't let anything bad happen. It's like playing hide-and-seek; the front porch or the maple tree was home base and when you made it to home base, you were always safe. My family was always my home base.

I guess I'm just old now and out of touch with the times. But when I hear about or see on the news that young kids have to have medications and therapies to deal with all their anxiety and fears, I think that maybe they need to be kids. Perhaps they need parents who aren't as concerned with providing all the conveniences money can buy or pushing them to be sports superstars or to achieve successes before they reach puberty. Maybe less social media and video games and more running and falling and skinning up their knees, then learning to get up by themselves, would help. Perhaps they just need a front porch, or a big maple tree, to call home base, where they know they are always safe.

Chapter 3
Milking the Cat

As you grow up, you go through different stages with your parents. As a child, we believe they are the most brilliant people ever. Then we become a teenager and we think we're the most intelligent people ever and our parents are the dumbest. Finally, you reach adulthood, have your own children, and realize you had it right the first time; your parents were the smartest.

Dad wasn't a strict disciplinarian; that was Mom. But Dad had his rules and expectations. There were consequences if you broke the rules or didn't live up to the expectations. But he did let us learn our lessons the hard way too, by trying and failing. He figured, "Well, I have four sons; the stupid ones will weed their selves out." He allowed us to have fun, but when it was time to work, it was time to work. There was none of this, "I'm sick," "I have a stomach ache," or "I have a headache." What castor oil and an aspirin wouldn't cure, a belt or a switch on the backside would. He was an early riser, and I hated that. None of us boys were early risers. Never were and never will be. On a Saturday when we were out of school, and there was work to be done, you got called to get up once.

"I'll give you boys just five minutes to get up and get ready," he'd open the door and say. There was no snooze button, and in five minutes, if you weren't up, you got a glass of cold water in the face. Then you got dressed and had to clean up the mess the water made. My oldest brother, Gary, learned to swim that way.

But working with Dad was fun. He would always joke or pull pranks. Dad was a master storyteller and always had a story. His stories were how I first developed my love of storytelling. When he told a story, he had a straight poker face. He would engage and allow you to use your imagination to become part of the story. It could be the most outrageous, unbelievable story, but when he finished, he left you asking yourself, "Is that really true? Did that really happen?" And, he never would tell you; he'd grin and say, "What do you think?" and leave it at that. Then I would spend the rest of the day bugging him to tell me if it was true, but all I ever got was, "What do you think?"

As I mentioned earlier, we had an assortment of animals, including some barn cats. I had this particular cat I was pretty fond of and named her Elsa. I had seen a movie on the *Wonderful World of Disney* television program from 1966 called *Born Free*. The film was about a lady named Joy Adamson, who rescued a female lion in Africa and named the lioness Elsa. My Elsa was the most affectionate of the several barn cats and followed me everywhere. One day, Elsa had a litter of kittens. She was an excellent mother, constantly cleaning and feeding her babies. For whatever reason, the kittens got sick after a few weeks, and the whole litter died. For the next several days, Elsa mopped around, constantly meowing for her kittens. One day, she hardly would move at all. She was lying around crying. I picked her up to inspect her and see what was wrong.

Let me throw in a little disclaimer right here before I continue. Certain words used on the farm might not be proper to use in polite company. Some might find them offensive. If that's you, jump past this chapter because I'm about to use the words "tits" and "nipples." Yes, I could use udders and teats, but that's for large livestock like cows and goats. I guess I could be proper and use the word mammary glands, but I've never been on a farm and heard the words "mammary glands" used in any form or fashion. Our dogs and cats always had tits and nipples; those are the words I'm going to use. Also, no mammary glands were injured in the writing of this chapter; now, back to the story.

When I picked Elsa up, I felt something strange on her bottom side. I flipped her over to look. Her tits were so swollen they looked like they were about to burst. I touched them, and they felt like they were on fire. Elsa let out a meow and hissed at me. I knew she was in pain and thought she must be sick like her kittens that died. I loved this cat, and it brought tears to my eyes to think of her death, but I didn't know what to do. Then I thought of Dad. Dad would know what to do. He was always doctoring sick animals. Surely if anyone could save Elsa's life, my dad could. I took Elsa and ran off to look for him. I found him in the garage sharpening mower blades with a grinder. I took Elsa, put her on top of the deep freezer, rolled her over on her back, and shouted, "Dad, come here, quick, and look how big Elsa's tits are!"

Dad finished his sharpening, shut the grinder off, and yelled back, "What?"

"Elsa's sick! Come see how big her tits are!"

I'm pretty sure that Dad felt, at the time, that if one of his sons were going to weed their way out of his pack of sons by doing stupid things, it would be me. But, when one of your children says, "Come see how big the cat's tits are," you have to look. Dad came over to the freezer; I spun Elsa over on her back so Dad could see.

Dad did just like I had; he reached down and touched Elsa's milk bags and felt how hot they were. She squirmed and meowed in pain. Dad sighed, shook his head, and said, "She's got milk fever because her kittens died, and she didn't dry up."

"Well, what's going to happen to her?"

"She's probably going to die if you can't get that milk out of her."

"Well, how do I milk her?"

"You know how to milk. Just milk her," Dad replied.

"You can milk a cat?" I asked.

Many years later, while watching a movie called *Meet the Fockers*, I realized that Robert DeNiro stole my Dad's line when Dad said, "Son, you can milk anything that has milk and nipples." He then continued, "I can hardly breathe. I've got to put some nose drops in my nose and put these blades back on the mower." Dad left Elsa and me in the garage to figure out this milking conundrum.

Dad was right. I knew how to milk. My cousin Gene had taught me. He was the best milker ever. He even showed me how to point the cow's nipple to shoot the milk in the air and watch the barn cats leap up to catch it in their mouths.

Milking is a fine art. You don't just start grabbing and tugging on a nipple like a sixteen-year-old teenager in the backseat of a 1970 Pontiac LeMans parked in the dark at the Star-lit drive-in. You must caress it with your thumb and forefinger up high, next to the milk bag. You gently pull down and squeeze your forefinger and thumb together to trap the milk in the nipple, and then use your other three fingers to squeeze and express the milk out of the nipple into the awaiting milk bucket.

I stood Elsa up on the freezer like she was a cow. I reached up and started to try and milk her. It wouldn't work. Even being only nine years old, my fingers and thumb were too large for her tiny cat nipples. I wasn't getting any milk and only hurting Elsa, who was trying to scratch me. I had to stop and think.

I looked out of the garage across the road to Baxter's Dairy. They milked many cows, but they didn't do it by hand. They used electric milkers that would attach to all four of the cow's nipples and use suction to express the milk. I knew I couldn't use the electric milker. They would never fit and would probably suck the cat's guts out. I don't think Baxter's would have let me use a milker to milk my cat anyway. That's when the light bulb came on. Dad's nose drop's dropper.

My dad was a nose drop addict. He had a sinus condition and started using nose drops to help him breathe and became addicted to it. His drug of choice was Neo-Synephrine. Back in those days, it didn't come in a spray bottle. It came in a brown-colored glass bottle that had a glass tube with a rubber bulb on top which also served as the cap to the bottle. You pull the glass tube out of the bottle, squeeze the rubber bulb to force the air out, insert the glass tube back in the bottle, and release the rubber bulb. As the air causes the bulb to expand, it creates a suction that would draw the liquid nose drops back up in the glass tube. You put the tip of the glass dropper in your nose, squeeze the rubber bulb, and shoot the drops into your nostril. It works by the same principle as the electric milkers at Baxter's Dairy farm.

I could hear Dad back working on the mower outside the garage, so I slipped into the house and into his bedroom. I took the glass dropper out of the nose drops and then snuck back to the garage with Elsa. I rolled her over, squeezed that black rubber bulb, and guided that glass tube carefully down over her little cat nipples. It fit perfectly, not too big, not too small, just like the Neo-Synephrine company had used a little cat nipple as a production model. I milked Elsa down that evening and expressed the milk I drew out of her in an old glass pickle jar. I was so relieved as I thought she might live. From the sound of Elsa's purring, she was enjoying it too while I milked her. She perked up, and it was like instant relief to her. After I finished, I took the dropper and put it back in the bottle on the headboard of Dad's bed.

I never told Dad what I was using to milk Elsa. I think he had forgotten all about her milk fever until a few weeks later when he walked into the garage. He saw me with Elsa on her back on top of the freezer.

"What in the Sam-hell are you doing, son?" That was a reoccurring phase I often heard Dad say to me growing up.

"I'm milking the cat so she won't die."

"Is it working?" Dad asked, standing there in disbelief

I held up the clear glass pickle jar and swirled it around so he could see the milk in the bottom while I hid the glass dropper in my other hand. "What do you think? She's getting better every day!" I exclaimed.

The shocked look Dad gave me when I said that confused me. I couldn't tell if he was ashamed of his son, who had a cat on its back on a deep freezer milking it, or if he was proud that I would do what he said would work and milk a cat to save its life. Maybe he was a little of both, but he gave me a big ole grin, shook his head in disbelief, and turned and walked out of the garage.

Nature's instinct began to kick in, and over the next few weeks, Elsa started to wean me off milking her just like she would have done her kittens if they had lived. Elsa dried up, and she was healthy and happy. I was delighted, and I even think Dad was happy because he soon stopped complaining about the awful smell his nose drops had been leaving in his nose recently. I guess I had forgotten to rinse the droppers out after I had used them.

The one regret I always had after my Dad died many years later was I never told him that I had used his nose dropper to milk the cat. The prankster in him would have appreciated it. I almost did one time. I was on vacation and visiting him at his home in Kentucky. I was about to walk out the backdoor and saw him sitting with a stray cat in his lap. He was sharing his bologna sandwich with it while he stroked its back and talked to the cat. He always pretended he didn't like cats. I knew if I opened the door and stepped out, he would throw the cat off his lap and act mad about it hanging around. I could tell by how big the cat was it had shared a lot of sandwiches with Dad. I stood there watching and thinking he would have milked the cat to save its life too. He loved animals, and he passed that on to his sons. I just backed slowly away from the door and let Dad enjoy his moment with the cat. I changed my mind about telling him, thinking it's best just to let sleeping cats lie. What do you think?

Chapter 4

My Dad—Pilot, Movie Director, and Catfish Resurrector

My dad's name was Tip Mink. He was born in 1927 in an area called Long Branch in the hills of Rockcastle County, Kentucky. He lived on the side of a hill across the creek from the Long Branch schoolhouse, which sat on a hill on the other side. Dad did walk to school and back uphill both ways barefooted, at least when he attended school. He dropped out in sixth grade to help work on the farm.

Although Dad only had a fifth grade education, I realize how smart he was now that I'm older. He could take almost anything apart, fix it, and put it back together. He could build almost anything you could think of with a plan inside his head; no instructions, no YouTube videos or internet tutorials. He'd used plain old common sense know-how based on necessity, because we were poor.

In his limited free time, if he wasn't playing his guitar or coon hunting, it was common to see him reading from an encyclopedia. "You're never too old to learn something, either by mistakes or by education. Education is easier but less likely," he'd say, always looking at me when he would say that.

Later in life, Dad even learned to pilot a plane, although he almost fell out of it once. My mom thought it would be a good idea to spell out his name, "TIP," with diapers in the front yard on one of his flyovers. Dad thought it would be a good idea to bank the airplane on its side and take a picture of his name spelled out in the yard. The pilot's side door of the airplane thought it was a good idea to open when he banked the airplane on its side. The camera he was holding thought it was a good idea to hurl to the ground from a thousand feet in the air as he tried to pull the door back shut. And me, well, I thought it was a good idea to run. Mom asked why I ran off and left my brother sitting by himself on one of the diapers. I replied, "Because he likes his picture taken!" From the look Mom gave me when I said that, saying that was not a good idea.

Fortunately, Dad had fastened his seat belt before taking off. The camera missed everyone. And fortunately, before my mom could smack my smart mouth, my little brother pooped and began wallowing around in it. Mom grabbed the "I" in "TIP" to change him, which left a big "TP" shining up at Dad, who was still flying above us trying to get his door closed. Even at six years of age I thought it was ironic my little brother had pooped and we had TP'd our own yard. Mom was mad, for quite a while, about the camera. When Dad got home, Mom asked him why he dropped her camera. He replied, "I'm sorry, I didn't have time to put a parachute on it;

I was trying not to fall to my death." I got my smart mouth honest. That ended Dad's pilot days. For years afterward, whenever I would find a piece of the camera wreckage, Dad would tell me to go bury it and not mention it to Mom.

My two oldest brothers were often gone doing teenage stuff like girls or cars and later gone to the marines and the navy. By now, a lot of my cousins had grown up and moved off. When he wasn't pooping in the yard or eating dirt, my youngest brother was usually with Mom. After Dad had ended the club initiations and until I was around twelve years old, I was always Dad's little tagalong. When he was working on something, I was right there. It was usually to fetch him something and sometimes to hold on to a sparkplug wire to see if the engine had any fire.

If you have never placed one hand on the end of a sparkplug wire and the other hand on the top of a sparkplug and felt the electrical current caress your body while your dad turns over the engine, then you never lived, or at least in my childhood anyway. When I had a massive heart attack years later, and the emergency room doctors couldn't restart my heart with the electric paddles, I blamed it on all the sparkplug wire holding, peeing on electric fences, and Annette Funicello for making me immune to electricity. That's my theory of the paddles' ineffectiveness in reviving me and why my sternum got cracked by the ER doctor punching me in the chest administering the cardio thump. Medical science may disagree.

Speaking of theories, I must have gotten my theory trait from my dad. Although Dad was brilliant with plenty of common sense, he also had many ideas involving life's great mysteries. As his sidekick and tagalong, somehow, I always felt my duty was to disprove those I thought were wrong. Sometimes he would agree, but most times, I got a love tap on the back of the head with a "Shut up, smartass, I'm trying to think."

Long before video recorders, phone cameras, and the like, in the late 1960s, 8mm movie cameras were the state of the art in home moviemaking. My dad saved up and bought an 8mm movie camera and projector to make home movies. If you had an 8mm and later a Super 8mm home movie camera, you were somebody in our family, and my dad became somebody.

Dad would film anyone and everything – family, friends, horses, coon dogs. But his favorites were natural disasters, especially floods and tornados. Natural disasters were his favorites because no sound was required. These old movies had no sound, and you didn't need sound to grasp the effect of a flood or the aftermath of a storm. With family and friends, it was primarily awkward smiles and waving and trying to read their lips of what they were saying.

During the 1960s, the film had to be taken to a drug store and sent off for development. It usually took a week or more to get the developed film back. Then a big movie debut, which would rival Hollywood's, would occur in our living room. The movie premiers always happened on a Friday evening. Dad got paid every Friday and had to wait until payday to get the film out of the drugstore and buy new film for the next movie.

On premier Friday, our kitchen chairs were set out in the living room in rows. He would set up the projector and screen. Mom would make popcorn, and we would all take our seats and wait for dark. When Dad had judged the living room was dark enough to illuminate the movie on the white sheet hung on the wall, Dad would say, "Okay, here we go. Lights. Camera. Action!"

Of course, about the time he said "action," someone would say, "Hold on, I've got to pee." Everyone in the living room would let out an irritated sigh. Then we'd all wait in the dark living room while everyone took turns emptying their bladders, well, all except us kids. We knew it was better to pee our pants than to hold the movie up.

The film would only last about five minutes; then, everyone would sit around and critique how well they smiled, grinned, and waved in the film. Dad later learned to combine small movies by splicing them together and making more significant half-hour extravaganzas. When the color film became available for the 8mm cameras, Dad was beside himself with excitement. This colorization would take his home moviemaking productions to another level. Now everyone could smile, wave, and grin in living color. He could hardly wait to test out his newest theory, which turned into a massive debate between him and me.

We went to my grandma's in Maud one Sunday, as we often did after she got home from church. This visit would often turn into a religious debate between my dad and his sisters about who was going to hell over having music in church. My dad thought God didn't care one way or another, and my aunts disagreed. My mom took my brother and me to a Pentecostal church, so I never knew there were churches without music. On this particular Sunday, however, Dad brought his movie camera loaded with the color film to test his newest theory. Hanging on my grandma's living room wall were two 8*10 pictures of my oldest brother, Gary, taken in the marines. One photo was in black and white, and the other was him in color, wearing his dress blue uniform. Dad first started filming the picture of my brother in his dress blues, and then slowly panned across the wall to film the black-and-white photograph.

"Now, when I get this color film developed, that black-and-white picture of Gary will be in color just like the other one," Dad said.

"No, it won't. It's going to be just like the one on the wall," I said, smiling and waving because he was pointing the camera at me.

"You watch and see, smartass."

"Tip, it's Sunday. Don't be cussing!" Grandma scolded Dad.

"What do I have to lose? I believe the Lord likes music in church," Dad replied.

Dad and I debated the black-and-white versus the color film all week. Neither one of us was backing down from our beliefs. When the debate became too heated, and I was nearing a smack behind the head, I would change the subject and say, "You're right, Dad. God likes music too."

Finally, payday came and it was time to get the film from the drugstore. We dragged the kitchen chairs into the living room. Dad hung the sheet on the wall and set the projector up. We all took turns peeing and sat in our assigned seats, ate our popcorn, and waited for dark. Finally, it was time, and Dad said, "Lights, camera, action!"

The movie started, and there were my aunts who didn't like music in church, smiling and waving in their living-color church dresses. The film panned to my grandma, smiling and waving, spitting the snuff she had in her mouth into her spit can. The movie then shifted and focused on the wall behind my grandma. It began panning to the left ever so slowly until it came to my brother Gary's colorized portrait in his marine dress blues and stopped.

"That picture looks crooked, Cordie," my mom said to my grandma, sitting in the audience.

"There must be something wrong with the nail. I straighten that thing every day, and it goes right back to leaning," Grandma replied.

"Shhh! It's almost to it," Dad said.

"Tip, can you fix that nail next time you're at the house?" Grandma asked.

"Yes! Yes! I'll fix the nail." Dad said, getting exasperated from all the talking.

The movie started panning back to the left across the purple-flowered wallpaper of my grandma's living room. The tension was building in the room as the film was about to decide if Dad's theory was correct. At this point during the actual filming, we had forgotten about the fact; as the movie was about to reach the black-and-white picture of my brother Gary, my other brother Terry, who had been at Grandma's that day, had gotten up and walked in front of the camera as Dad was filming. Of course, like everyone else, Terry had stopped and smiled and waved at the camera while blocking out the black-and-white picture hanging behind him on the wall.

"Well, shit!!! Get the hell out of the way, Terry!" Dad screamed.

"Tip!!!" Grandma exclaimed.

"He can't hear you, Dad. It's a movie," I added.

"Shut up, smartass!"

It was like déjà vu because Dad must have yelled the same thing at Terry while filming this masterpiece. As soon as Dad yelled that in real time, Terry stopped smiling and waving in the movie and abruptly moved out of the frame. And there, behind where Terry had been standing, on the wall amidst the wallpaper with the purple flowers was hanging the black-and-white photo of Gary, still in black and white. Dad let out a deep sigh. I didn't say a word. I felt terrible for Dad. From the sadness of Dad's sigh, I would have rather been wrong.

"I guess you're right, son. So much for that theory."

"I still think Jesus likes music!" I blurted out, trying to make Dad feel better, which only incited an argument in the living room between the Pentecostals and the Church of Christ.

We never discussed black-and-white versus colorized film again. And although that idea didn't pan out, it never stopped Dad from having his theories.

Two of my Dad's brothers-in-law lived close by and in the summer would often come and go fishing with Dad in the pond. On one such occasion, the subject of fish freezing came up. Dad was developing a theory concerning what happens to the fish in the winter when the pond freezes over.

"You boys ever notice when the ice freezes over a pond in the wintertime, sometimes you'll see a fish frozen underneath the ice?" Dad asked.

"Yep, I have," Uncle Lovil said.

"Me too," Uncle James replied, and then added, "I've even cut them out of the ice and eaten 'em."

"Were they still good?" Uncle Lovil asked.

"Good enough to eat, the best I can remember."

"But, did you ever notice that when the ice thaws, there's never any dead fish floating?" Dad asked, already forming a theory in his mind.

"Nope, never did," Uncle James said.

"Me either," Uncle Lovil added.

"I think that when the water turns cold, the fish go into some type of hibernation, sort of like bears, and then they freeze and when the water warms back up, they come out of hibernation and back to life," Dad said.

"Sounds possible to me," Uncle Lovil said.

"I remember it was so cold in the war that a fella got shot in the leg, and his blood froze over and kept him from bleeding to death," Uncle James added. Uncle James had been a World War II veteran and had fought during the frozen Battle of the Bulge before being captured by the Germans.

The conversation continued about the possibilities of what would happen to the frozen fish. No one was catching any fish except me. I had landed a couple of nice-sized catfish and had put them on the stringer but was planning on throwing them back in the pond because I hated cleaning catfish. That was one of Dad's rules. You catch 'em; you clean 'em. He was the same towards hunting and would say to me, "If you kill it, you clean and eat it. Animals were put here for a purpose, not just so you can go around and kill something." I was about to take them off the stringer and throw them back in the pond when Dad said, "Don't throw them back."

"There's not enough to eat, and I don't want to clean them."

"Are they alive?"

"Yes."

"Good," Dad said. "Bring them to the house. I'm going to try an experiment. And don't roll your eyes at me."

When we returned to the house, Dad took the catfish off the stringer and threw them into the deep freezer. Then he said to my uncles, "We'll let them freeze good and solid for a week or so, and then we'll thaw them out in a washtub and see if they come back to life."

"Never going to work," I said under my breath as I watched the two catfish flop around on top of the frozen bags of corn. Dad slammed the freezer door shut before they flopped out.

"You don't know, smartass," Dad said, giving me a little love tap behind my head to let me know he had heard me or at least knew what I was thinking.

I could hear the poor catfish flopping around in the freezer for the next hour. I would open the freezer, and Dad would hear the freezer door squeak and scold me, "Shut that damn freezer and leave those fish alone." I quietly opened the freezer and checked on the fish a few more times without him hearing me. The last time I checked, the catfish had peace- fully succumbed to their life of tranquility on top of ripped bags of corn and strawberries.

Finally, a week later, my uncles came to the house for the anticipated day of the catfish resurrection. My Dad got a big washtub and filled it with water. He brought the two frozen, stiff catfish out of the freezer, cursing under his breath about the mess they had made with the corn and the strawberries. He placed them in a large nine-gallon washtub filled with warm water. Dad and my uncles pulled the kitchen chairs out into the garage and placed them around the washtub. There they began a vigil of watching fish thaw.

They smoked cigarettes, chewed tobacco, drank a few beers, and talked during the vigil. They spoke about their youth in Kentucky. They talked about work. Uncle Lovil retold the story about riding past a graveyard late one night and an owl swooping down and taking his hat off. He about ran his mule to death across Pongo Ridge, trying to outrun the ghost that kept flogging him in the head as he rode. Uncle Lovil, after all those years, was still unsure if it was a ghost from the graveyard or a hoot owl from a tree. "Both can fly," he laughed and said.

Uncle James told about how cold and hungry he was in the German prisoner-of-war camp. He spoke of how he would dig for grubs and worms to eat and, on a good day, catch a rat.

"A rat looks just like a squirrel when you skin it, and they taste almost similar too," Uncle James said as he bent his tall, gangly frame in the chair and poked the catfish, checking on their degree of thaw, but his eyes were still looking back to 1945 in Germany.

Dad spoke about his grandpa, who had told him that he would give Dad his farm when he died if Dad would stay and live with him in Kentucky. Dad told him no and said he was tired of working on the farm, busting rocks and dirt, trying not to starve. Dad moved to Cincinnati when he was nineteen years old and worked in the factories and later drove trucks, but he always missed Kentucky.

"At least when I'm driving, I feel like I'm going somewhere. Maybe going home," he said sadly.

He reached and felt the catfish. Feeling they were completely thawed, he declared disappointedly, "I think they're dead, boys, and they ain't coming back to life."

That's when I blurted out what I'd wanted to say during this whole two-hour catfish resurrection vigil, "Did you ever think they suffocated to death long before they ever froze to death?"

"Did you ever think you need to start cleaning that mess out of the freezer, smartass?" The look Dad gave me when he said that made me think the fish may have been thawed, but I was skating on thin ice. But Uncle James, as he often did, came to my rescue.

"You know, Tip, I think the boy is onto something. When those fish freeze in the pond, they're in water and breathing. We should have frozen 'em in that tub of water.

"That's right," Uncle Lovil agreed, then added, "and brim and blue-gill always freeze on top. Catfish stay at the bottom. We need to try it with some brim and bluegill in a tub of water."

"Then next week, boys, we'll catch us some bluegill and brim!" Dad exclaimed with new hope, then he looked at me with a softer look in his eyes and said, "And you still need to clean out that freezer, smartass."

Thinking back, I learned a lot that day. I learned Uncle James was a true American hero and survived when many would have given up and quit. I learned Uncle Lovil was afraid of owls and ghosts, but he faced and laughed at his fears. And I learned from my dad it's okay to have theories and think outside the box. Even when you're wrong, you can always learn something, and the important thing is always to learn.

Dad and my uncles never did try the experiment with the brim and bluegill, or if they did, I wasn't privy to it. I'd often check the freezer for a tub of frozen fish, but all there were was the usual stuff and some loose pieces of corn and strawberries I'd missed. I've thought of going fishing and repeating the experiment, but then it's best just left alone and to think Dad and my uncle's theory was correct. Now that I'm older, I've realized that Dad was always right and me, well, I was always a smartass.

Chapter 5

Discipline and Damn Onions

My parents believed in "spare the rod and spoil the child." By today's standards, my dad and mom would probably have been arrested for child abuse. They weren't child abusers. I never was punched or kicked or tortured. My parents spanked me with a firm hand, a switch, or a belt. The switch usually came from one I was sent to pick out and fetch for the whipping. I had better not bring back some flimsy or rotten one either. I was taught not to lie and not to disrespect others or other people's property. I'm going to write something now that some won't agree with or will make some angry. In my opinion, you can correlate the lack of respect for others and others' property with the lack of discipline a child receives growing up.

Once, when I was nine years old, I went to the Crossroads store with my mom. She wouldn't buy me a candy bar, so I put it in my pocket when no one was looking. Once in the car, I was stupid enough to pull it out and was about to start eating it. My mom jerked me and the candy bar out of the car and whipped me back into the store. I had to put the candy bar on the counter, explain to the lady I had stolen it, and apologize. The lady didn't coddle me; she read me the riot act. My mom then paid for the candy bar and whipped me back to the car. She promptly opened the candy bar she had paid for and ate it in front of me, explaining all the way home about the evil of taking something that didn't belong to me. When I got home, I got sent to bed to think about what I had done.

Mom did the majority of the disciplining. Dad was gone a lot driving a semitruck, and she saved the big stuff for him and his truck driving belt. I got the most whippings for some reason. The reasons were usually due to my brothers because I was the perfect child. My younger brother, Ron, did something one day, and Mom got after him with a switch. He took off running for dear life. Instead of chasing him, Mom just yelled, "You have to go to sleep sometime!" She turned and returned to the house. Later, we came in, and everything was normal. Mom never mentioned the switching. That night, Ron and I got in bed together and went to sleep. We both thought she had forgotten. Mom was much younger then and, apparently, didn't develop dementia until much later in life because when we fell sound asleep, Mom busted in the room with the switch. The light flipped on, Mom ripped back the covers, and she blistered my brother's behind, saying, "I told you you'd have to sleep sometime!" I rolled over, closed my eyes, and tried to become invisible. Suddenly, she started switching me. I yelled, "What did I do?"

"Probably something I don't know about," as she pulled the covers back over us, turned the light off, and said, "Now go to sleep."

Another time, when Ron was just a toddler, he came up missing. Dad and Mom were all in a panic and began looking for him. They called relatives and neighbors to come help in the search. They checked all through the back fields, the pond, and the barn, all the way down to Gregory Creek, yelling and calling for him. Dad told me to stay at the house in case he came back. I was sitting on a bench on the back porch, bent over, praying for my little brother's safe return. Before I could say amen, I heard a little snicker. I listened closer and heard the "Hee hee hee" snicker again. I bent further down and looked between my legs under the bench. There was my little brother, with a big circle of dirt around his mouth, squatting as low as he could, hiding, snickering, and watching everyone search frantically for him.

I jumped off the bench and began yelling as loudly as possible, "Here he is! I found him!" Then I looked under the bench and told little Mud Mouth, "You're going to get a whipping." I was sure I would be hailed as a hero for finding him. Everyone came running back to the house. They all took turns hugging Ron and telling him how worried they were. No one said anything to the hero who had found him. After everyone left, Mom told me to cut a switch. I got a good one for her to whip Ron. I handed her the switch, and she grabbed my arm, and we did the little circle switching dance together while I was saying, "But I found him," and she would reply, "But you lost him." She was correct; he had been my responsibility. I was the older brother. I decided then and there that I would never allow Mud Mouth to join any clubs I formed as my older brothers had let me.

The worse whipping I got all started when I was a young teenager when I said, "I ain't planting no more damn onions!" That's what I said as I threw the onion sets down and started out of the garden. As I mentioned, there were certain words you could say on the farm that weren't considered profanity, like nipples and tits with the cat story. I could even say shit instead of manure when cleaning stalls; it all depended on the context and the company that was present. But damn, no, sir, there was no context we kids were allowed to say that.

What could have possessed me to say something like that? Sometimes, thinking back, I still wonder. I blame it on hormones. I was in the early stages of some rather long, tedious teenage years and feeling my oats. During my thirteenth summer of life, I had become a man, and the little stick girl that lived next door had blossomed into a woman, boobies and all. I knew Dad wouldn't understand that I had a pre-planned rendez-vous to keep with the newly blossomed, former stick girl that lived next door, and his onion planting was about to mess all that up.

I was just about to step out of the last row and was thinking, "Hmmm, I had made it over four rows of freshly planted onions, and I hadn't heard anything back from Dad, so I guess he knows I mean business." In hind-sight, it wasn't that at all. Dad was so shocked at what I had said that he had to stop and think for a minute if he had heard what he thought he had heard. I guess he decided he had heard me correctly, and that's when I heard the most dreaded of all of Dad's favorite sayings, "Oh yes, BUT you are!" with the emphasis on "but." I hated when he said, "Oh yes, BUT you are!" That was Dad's no nonsense, no compromise, no negotiations, no trade-offs, no arguments. Nothing but "oh yes, BUT you are," of doing whatever he had said to do.

It had to have been hormones. That's the only explanation I can think of—that damned testosterone. Testosterone has been a curse of mine my whole life. I can pinpoint every bad thing that has ever occurred in my life, and it always leads back to one source, testosterone. And although I remember trying to stop myself, that damn testosterone wouldn't let me, and I yelled right back to him, "Oh NO, BUT I'm not!" Instead of just stressing the "but," as Dad did, I threw in extra stress on the "no" just for good measure. I'm not sure why I felt I needed to throw that additional stress in there because I knew it was a mistake as it came out of my mouth. Just like stopping at the garden's edge and looking back was a mistake.

Let me stop here and preface something. I read somewhere that the second-biggest drive in a man is the sex drive. Like I said before, that dang testosterone causes the drive that creates almost every problem a man has had or ever will have. That sex drive pushes him to do stupid, stupid things, not only to do stupid, stupid things but to say stupid, stupid things. However, that is drive number two, second only to man's number one drive. His will to survive.

I can confirm this is true. Because when I turned and saw Dad coming down the row of onions that I had just set out, watching the little white bulbs being stomped into the freshly tilled soil under his boots as he unbuckled his belt, I suddenly forgot about my rendezvous with my beautiful, newly blossomed, former stick girl next door and broke into a full sprint.

I had about ten good steps and was almost up to full speed when I heard the other dreaded phrase, "You better come back here, or you're gonna get it worse!" Dad's "gonna get it worse" was much worse than Mom's "you got to sleep sometime." With Mom's, at least you didn't know it was coming. With Dad, you knew it was coming. This day was just one mistake compounded by another, compounded by yet another mistake; believing that I could "get it worse" and stopping just long enough to let Dad get within grabbing distance of me.

I'm sure others have been beaten worse than I was that day, but I've yet to meet them. At that time, Dad was a truck driver and wore one of those big leather belts with his name, Tip, embroidered in the middle of the belt, and at the end was a big brass buckle with a protruding image of a cab-over Kenworth semitruck. Even now, if I look at my bare rear end in a mirror, I can almost see my Dad's name on one cheek and the image of a cab-over Kenworth on the other. And yes, oh BUT YES, I did plant onions that day, and I planted and planted until there were no onions left to plant. And yes, But Yes, I did get to plant a kiss on my newly, beautifully blossomed former stick girl next door one late summer evening weeks later, but to my disappointment, she had "onion breath."

I thought about that day years later when I was planting my garden. I wasn't thinking about the whipping; I was thinking about something I learned that day. One of those things you know but you don't remember learning it. It just becomes a part of you. It's the virtues of hard work, persistence, and respect. It was always a proud moment when folks told me how respectful and hardworking my children were. Let me brag for a moment; they get it from their upbringing, just like I did. It's one of the family traditions you must pass down if you want it to survive, and like me, it's usually learned the same way, the hard way. That's the worst I ever remember my Dad whipping me.

Today, the state and family services would have locked him up, but I learned a lesson in discipline that day that has been with me all my life. The same discipline makes me sit and write when I'd rather play. The same discipline that made me get up in the mornings and go to work at those phosphate mines for thirty-eight years, providing for my family. It's that same discipline that taught me to respect others and the property of others. I'm reminded of the proverb that says, "Train up a child in the way he should go; and when he is old, he will not depart from it."

Many years later, when my dad was in his seventies, my family and I visited him on vacation in Kentucky at the same home where I now live. It was always his favorite story. We sat outside under a big maple tree, talking and watching my kids run and play and laughing about the onion story. My Dad was watching the kids, and suddenly he got very quiet and serious, and said, "You sure surprised me, son."

"I did? How's that?" I asked.

"I never figured you'd be one of my sons to settle down and raise a family of such fine young'uns."

"Why do you say that?"

"Because, son, you were always wild and crazy. I didn't think you'd live to see thirty years old."

"I thought Gary was the wild and crazy one?" I asked.

"Gary was just wild; you were wild and crazy. You always marched to your own tune. If somebody dared you to do something or told you couldn't do something, you'd do it or bust trying."

"Well, I did bust several times, Pops. But I learned, and I never gave up. You taught me that."

With that, Dad stood up and turned to go into the house. But before he left, he put his hand on my shoulder, and with a squeeze, he said, "You did good. I'm proud of you, son." He had never said anything like that to me before.

A few years ago, after I had bought my Dad's old home, I planted a garden in the same spot he always gardened, including setting out onions. I sat under the same maple tree where Dad and I had watched my kids play twenty years prior. As a light Kentucky evening breeze was revitalizing my tired body; I looked across the garden at the onions I had planted. I thought about what Dad had said that day as he squeezed my shoulder. With a smile on my face and tears dripping down on my cheeks, I said out loud, "I'm proud of you too, Dad, but I still hate planting those damn onions."

Section Two
Tales from Momma's Dungeon

Chapter 6

Transition to the Dungeon

No longer a fugitive: Me, Mom, and Ron,
Christmas 1977 after my return to Florida

W e moved to Florida when I was sixteen years old. My life
transitioned many times over the next thirty-two years—
both of my lives. The one people saw and the one they didn't.
At eighteen, I had federal warrants issued for my arrest. I was wanted for
kidnapping, taking a minor across state lines with illegal intent, and statu-
tory rape. I kidnapped my first wife, Pam, who was fifteen at the time and
a ward of the State of Florida. I was eighteen. We hid in the mountains of

North Carolina. We lived in a migrant labor camp and worked packing apples under the alias names of Walter and Wendy Pind.

The living conditions in the camp were deplorable. We lived in a single-wide mobile home that had been subdivided into five apartments. Each apartment had a bunk bed mounted on the wall. There was a small sink, a toilet, and a stand-up shower. Meals were cooked over a hot plate inside or on a grill outside. When we had saved enough money, we went in half with the neighbors in the next apartment and bought a refrigerator that, due to lack of room, we sat outside between our apartments. We had to padlock it to keep others from stealing our food and drinks. The apartment was no bigger than a prison cell, but it didn't matter. It was mainly just for sleeping because we spent most of the time working in the apple crop.

In our free time, late in the evenings, the men would build a bonfire and sit around it and drink beer and tell stories. They spoke of adventures and hard times following and working the harvest throughout the country, usually starting in Florida, working oranges and cucumbers, then to the apples in North Carolina, sometimes tobacco in Tennessee and Kentucky, and then to cherries in Michigan. Sometimes the stories were told in English, sometimes in Spanish. Either way, I listened intently and took it all in.

The apple season ended abruptly in late September, and it was time to move on. Fortunately, the search for us had died down. During my time in North Carolina, I only had occasional contact with my Mom in Florida through a complex system of letter forwarding to and from relatives in Kentucky. This made it harder to trace the letters to Walter Pind, General Delivery, Edyneville, North Carolina. Like my ancestors before me, the hills and hollers of Southeast Kentucky began to call. Pam and I made our way to my aunt Gwen's in Kentucky.

We tried to get married in Tennessee, but the laws were stricter there than in Kentucky. Through a series of forgeries and frauds, Pam and I obtained a marriage license and were married on October 6, 1977 in

Livingston, Kentucky. At that point, if caught, I was already facing most of my life in prison, so what were a few more charges? Not wanting to stay in one place too long or entangle my relatives in my problems, Pam and I made our way to Ohio. My dream of attending college and becoming a best-selling author was gone.

My dad and mom had separated and were in the process of a divorce. My dad was living back in Ohio. After arriving in Ohio, my dad got me a job in a factory where he and my two oldest brothers worked. It was called Nachman and they made wooden frames for mattresses. I ran an air gun that shot nails into bed frames for $2.10 an hour. We rented an apartment in Mason, Ohio with only a table, two chairs, and a bed my cousin Debbie gave us. Our entertainment center was a twelve-inch black-and-white TV we had bought at a flea market in Ashville.

There was a police chief in Bowling Green, Florida, where my mom lived. His name was Doyle Bryan. Doyle always liked me for whatever reason and knew the whole story behind why I had come back to Florida and kidnapped Pam. He was working on my behalf to get the charges dropped. Doyle would stop by my mom's and say, "Now I know you don't know where he's at, but if you were to talk to him, tell him for me . . ." Then he would give her messages to relay to me. Doyle knew my mom knew where I was hiding out but never pressured her to tell. Finally, after Pam and I were married, he was successful. The State of Florida and the feds didn't want to be bothered with all the extradition and marriage annulment that would have been involved in bringing us back to Florida. They had bigger fish to fry than two young kids that no one seemed concerned with.

That winter in Ohio was one of the coldest on record. We could barely pay the rent and had little money for food. My mom contacted me and told me Doyle had gotten all the charges dropped. I was no longer a fugitive. I told Pam to pack up. We were going back to Florida. I thought, "If it's not true and I get arrested, at least I'll be warm and have food to eat."

My dad had to return to Florida for the divorce, so we loaded up and returned home. Doyle would later become the Hardee County sheriff. Years later, after I became a Christian, Doyle would invite me to come to the jail and minister and give my testimony to the prisoners. I always remembered what he had done for me and always obliged. He was one of the best men I've ever met.

Still, those early years after we returned to Florida were full of drug abuse and pack-muleing drugs. During the Chippendales craze in the 1980s, I made money dancing for a short period. This was the wild and crazy me. This was the me that my dad didn't think would live to be thirty years old. But at thirty, I got control of the wild and crazy me, but trying to morph the old me into the new me was a struggle at best. Pam and I would stay together for eleven years and have three sons. But marrying at such a young age finally took its toll, and we divorced.

In 1989 I married my second wife, Stephanie. It was love at first sight. We had a whirlwind affair and were married within a few months without ever really getting to know each other. This would later become our downfall. We would stay together for eighteen years and have two sons and a daughter. We had a happy marriage for most of those years. But, because we were so different, sometimes it would get bad, really bad. I would go into a deep, dark depression for days and weeks as memories haunted me. She would try to help, but she couldn't understand, and I couldn't explain it. This would only make things worse. I would say terrible things. The *Book of Proverbs* says, "Death and life are in the power of the tongue," and mine slowly killed our marriage.

During this time, I lived an everyday life. I was a husband. I was a father. I coached baseball and was always active in the community. I worked mainly at the phosphate mines. I was also Bowling Green, Florida's mayor and commissioner for twelve years. Through these periods, there would be many happy and good times followed by deep depression and despair. There were days when I felt like the worst husband and father ever, and that would only bring on more guilt and depression. To others, I was a happy, carefree man who had everything together, but God bless those two wives; they got to see the worst of me. There was always a struggle in my mind.

I had been an atheist, or at least agnostic. I didn't believe in God, or if he did exist, I didn't care. Everything I'd seen and done was always there to haunt me. Then one day in 1980, I had an "Apostle Paul on the Damascus Road" moment. The Lord met me one on one, and we had a long discussion. I accepted Jesus as my Lord and Savior, and that's when the old man and the new man really began to fight.

For many years, I had an on-again-and-off-again relationship with the Lord. Sometimes I would live a good Christian life for years, then something would trigger me, and the old man and the double life would return. I would think back to times when I narrowly escaped with my life. I thought it was luck or fate. Later, the Lord showed me his hand was intervening in my life. I would recall things where I had narrowly escaped with my life, like overdosing at seventeen on PCP, dying, being shown hell, and then being sent back. Or another time, having a rifle against my head, and the trigger pulled, but the rifle not firing. These things hadn't been luck or fate but prayers on my behalf being answered. I found it took much more faith to be an atheist than a follower of Christ.

I'm not turning this book into one of a religious theme, but as I said in the introduction, this story is about life and from my life, and that has been a big part of my life. The new man and the old man would fight for several years. There would be many dark periods where I would go into depression, mostly over guilt for the life I'd led and the things I'd done. Thoughts of suicide were always there. It's always easier to forgive others than to forgive yourself, and it is even harder to forget.

This chapter has been the hardest to write. I've written it several times and thought about not including it in the book, but it's an integral part of transitioning into the dungeon, and someone reading this right now needs to hear this. Although many people have been touched by suicide and mental health issues, few want to discuss it or recognize that it is becoming more prevalent. People hide it well because of the stigma surrounding it, and discussing it is almost taboo.

A physical illness is hard to hide; it's there for everyone to see. A mental illness like depression is much easier to hide, and I was a master at it. The deeper and darker the depression becomes, the more withdrawn a person becomes, preventing anyone from noticing. The more withdrawn one becomes, the more tunnel vision one has, and depression and despair consume the person until, finally, the only way of escape seems to be to end it all. It's like being caught in a whirlpool; the deeper you go, the faster and tighter the darkness grips you.

After my second wife and I split, the hurt, pain, and depression became unbearable. Many say suicide is selfish, but my mindset at the time was not selfishness. I was tired of trying to be the person I thought I should be. The ones I loved would be much better off without me.

Finally, one Friday evening after I got off work, I decided it was time. I went to my house, got some clothes and my pistol, and headed to the beach at Anna Marie Island, Florida, to end my suffering and that of everyone around me. I decided I would check into a bungalow on the beach that Friday evening, and Sunday, I would put the pistol in my mouth and pull the trigger. I went there because I would rather a stranger find my body than one of my loved ones.

I decided my suicide note would be a story chronicling the act instead of writing a little goodbye note. I would title the story, "Now I Lay Me Down to Sleep," from the prayer my mom had taught me when I was little. If you've never heard it, it goes like this. "Now I lay me down to sleep. I pray the Lord my soul to keep. If I should die before I wake, I pray the Lord my soul to take." That would be the last line of the story. Of course, I never finished the story and thought I had destroyed it, but while searching through old stories for this chapter, I found the file with the story on it. I won't include the whole file in this chapter; too much involves many personal things and other people, but I will put enough to allow you into my mindset at the time. Just a note here, I wrote the story in the third person. Here is the story.

Now I Lay Me Down to Sleep

He thought it was divine intervention when going to the Beach Inn popped into his mind, and he knew that was the place. It almost made him excited when the thought occurred, like they were going back again. He thought of all the memories during the hour-and-a-half drive to the beach. His heart sank when he arrived, only to find it torn down and a new modern resort in the process of being built in its place. "Par for the course," he thought as he worked his way out of the parking lot and back onto the street.

As he drove, he saw a vacancy sign at the White Sands Gulf Front Beach Resort. He pulled into the parking lot and walked to the office to check in, thinking to himself, "Looks like I have to settle for second place again." It wasn't the Beach Inn, the cozy little bungalow with the second-floor suite and a hot tub where they had stayed when she loved him, but it was next door, which would be as close as he could get.

He stood and waited for the older couple checking in ahead of him to finish. He envied them when they announced to him and the desk clerk that they had been married for forty-seven years and were there to celebrate her 70th birthday with a return trip to the White Sands. It had a deep meaning in their relationship too, as the Beach Inn had for him. For a moment, he forgot why he was there. He stood there wishing he could trade places with this couple for a day, even if it meant aging 20 years. It would be worth it to feel that happiness and joy again, even for one night.

The clerk drew him back to reality as the couple walked past, and he smiled at them and told the lady, "Happy Birthday."

"So, how long do you plan to be with us?" asked the desk clerk.

"Probably just one night," he replied, "maybe two."

"Okay, I'm going to put you in 9-A. It's empty tonight and not reserved for tomorrow night if you decide on a second night."

"Give me the second night too. I won't need a third," he said, hoping for a miracle, but he couldn't see that happening.

He took the key and went to his room. The room was very nice, all tropical and tourist decor. Much nicer than he needed, he thought to himself. He wasn't feeling tropical or touristy as he put his bag on the bed, took his .40 caliber Smith and Wesson semi-automatic, and laid it beside his laptop on the table. He poured a cup of coffee, sat it on the table with his cigarettes and lighter, and began to write . . .

No one wakes up one morning and says to themselves, "Hey, I think I'll kill myself." They probably might hit the snooze a few more times if they did. So, this day started like any other – oversleeping, rummaging around for something to wear, and then out the door, hoping to find a swallow or two of old coffee in the cup he had left in his truck. He had bought it the night before on his way home from work. He felt a slight relief as he felt the slosh in the Styrofoam cup as he pulled it from the cup holder.

He swallowed it slowly; it wasn't good, and it wasn't hot, but it was strong and would hold him till he could reach the convenience store at the end of town. He tried to calculate how much sleep he had had this morning. He estimated through his grogginess no more than an hour and a half. Not much, he thought, but at least it was more than the night before. He had stayed up late to get everything in order so it wouldn't be so hard on whomever would replace him. Once home, he still had time for a decent night's sleep but decided to clean the bedroom.

The last straw that pushed him over the edge was when he went through all the drawers and sorted through all the keepsakes that had been kept. Birthday cards, anniversary cards, ticket stubs, and hotel brochures from places previously stayed. He recalled all the happy memories until he found a bunch of photos stuck in a box, pictures at the beach with them, four and a half years ago near the beginning of what was to become the end.

He kept the pictures of the kids from that weekend. But all the others he ripped to shreds. He didn't want to leave any part of that horrible weekend or the past four and half years. He held the coffee cup upside down, trying to drain the last drop from the cup, thankful he was only a few more blocks from the store. "Why do I stay up? Why can't I sleep?" He wondered to himself. He pulled into the store and bought a fresh cup of coffee, but his mind was still on last night.

He had sat on the bed and looked at his kids' keepsakes. One son had made a clay handprint for him for Father's Day in Sunday school. He pressed his hand against the tiny impression and tried to remember when his son had been that small fourteen years earlier. There had been a baggy with hair from the different kids' first haircuts. Oh, how he longed for those days again!

He opened the door to 9-A, put his pistol and laptop on the table by the front window, and threw his bag on the bed. He made a cup of complimentary coffee, lit a cigarette, sat down at the table, and started typing on the keyboard. He heard a rumbling in the distance and stopped typing to listen closely. Suddenly, it occurred to him that the waves were crashing in, and it took him back to the good and bad times of his life.

But he was alone now, and even the sound of the waves couldn't keep that feeling from him. When he had thought about where he would do it earlier in the day, he wasn't sure where. He didn't want to do it at home. Things were bad enough there now already, he certainly didn't want to traumatize his kids more by doing the act in their own home. And he knew he couldn't even take the remote chance that she or his kids would find him. He didn't even want to do it in his county or close to there; he knew everyone would gossip and whisper about it. The cops and EMT who would arrive at the scene might know him from his political career, such as it had been. He had been around the cops and paramedics enough to know they would talk to one another about the details, what it looked like, how he did it; all would guess why and give their educated opinions. Eventually, he knew, some of the facts would get back to his family, and how great their pain would already be without details added to it. That's when he thought of the beach.

The rest of the story is far too personal and involves others, and part of the story is lost. But I included enough of it here for you to understand my mindset. I wrote this story all Friday night, Saturday, and into Saturday night. I wrote my heart out; I cried and wrote, and I cried some more, and I wrote some more. I wrote about all my feelings and all my thoughts and all the things that had happened, which had brought me to this point.

When I started the story, I was overcome with depression and darkness. It was like a dark cloud trying to envelop and carry me deeper into the darkness, leaving all hope behind. I couldn't think past that moment; tomorrow seemed an eternity away. But then, a strange thing happened: each time I wrote through an event, emotion, or feeling, the cloud would draw back further away from me. The darkness drew back further and further. I was writing fast, getting deep-seated feelings out. I outwrote the devil.

I never finished this story. I had written until Saturday night, and I had nothing left in me to write. I was drained. I lay on the bed, still made from when I arrived. I just felt numb. I no longer felt hopeless, but I still felt no hope. As I lay there, something a twelve-year-old kid I'd coached in Little League Baseball had said ten years before popped into my head. Don't forget to pray. So I repeated the little "Now I Lay Me Down to Sleep" prayer my mom had taught me. After the prayer, another thought occurred to me that the twelve-year-old had said: "Sometimes you just have to close your eyes and believe." So I closed my eyes. I fell fast asleep. The best sleep I had had in such a long time.

I awoke the following day, opened the door, and looked out at the Gulf of Mexico. I could see a tomorrow and more tomorrows. I walked out onto the beach that Sunday morning for the first time since I had checked in on Friday evening. I walked along the beach, listening to the surf for a while, and then returned to the room. I took the clip out of the pistol, racked the round out of the chamber, and put it back in the clip. I packed the gun and my belongings in the car and checked out of the room.

Before leaving, I decided to walk the beach again. As I walked along the beach, I knew I needed to get some help. The darkness was at bay, but I knew it would return. God gives us a free will to choose. I chose that day to live and get help. The next day, I called the employee assistance program at my job, and they connected me to a mental health therapist. I don't mean to stereotype here, but it's true; many men feel that seeing a mental health therapist is a weakness. Perhaps it is, but the first step to getting better is admitting that weakness to yourself. I was weak and broken; the only one who could fix me was me, but I needed someone to show me how.

Within a few days, through the employee assistance program, my job got me an appointment to see the lady who would become my mental health therapist for the next several years. On the first visit, I told her about the whole weekend at the beach. She suggested I move out of the big house, where I lived alone, and the memories associated with it for a while. I needed to be around someone, and I needed to continue to write.

Now, at almost fifty years of age, I had came full circle from the place where I had left when I was eighteen when I had journeyed off to hitchhike around the country to find experiences and stories to write. I packed up what I needed and my laptop and moved into my mom's back bedroom, which I lovingly called the dungeon. With guidance from Dorothy, my therapist, and all the wild interactions and adjustments from moving back into the dungeon, I began writing stories of everyday life with my mom. I started posting them in a blog on the old Myspace pages, and Tales from Momma's Dungeon, which was the concept for this book, began. The following chapters in this segment are some of those stories.

Chapter 7

Jesus, the Owl, and Baxter the Waterhead

Pictures from the Dungeon

Moving back to live with my mom was a culture shock. She still lived in the same little cracker-box house we had moved to in Florida when I was sixteen. The same place I couldn't wait to leave when I graduated high school. Nothing much had changed in the past thirty years. The only upgrade was Mom had a window air conditioner in the living room and another in her bedroom. The dungeon, where I was to stay, had none, and it was hotter than Satan's pepper patch. But I had grown up without air-conditioning, so I figured I could survive. The one thing I forgot was back then, I was a teenager and athletic; now I was almost fifty and fat.

The room looked the same as when its last resident, my son Caleb, had lived there. Caleb joined the army and did two and a half tours as a combat medic because he said, "It wasn't as hot in Iraq, and the living conditions were better than in the dungeon." He's the one that named the back bedroom the dungeon. The first thing on my list of improvements was a window air conditioner. It would take a while. When I paid child support and the bills, I usually had twenty or thirty dollars left until the next paycheck, two weeks away.

I would describe the room decor as "la piled with junk." The room was complete with 1970s paneling my dad had put up when we first moved there. There were one dresser and two chests of drawers, or as we say in the south, Chester drawers, which left just enough room to walk to the full-size bed in the corner. The bed and mattress were the same ones my younger brother and I had slept on as kids. To complete the ambiance, and tie the room's decor together, was an oil painting of an owl on the north wall. Not an ordinary painting, a giant, hideous painting of an owl. Directly across the room on the south wall was a picture of Jesus praying in the garden of Gethsemane. He was sweating great drops of blood, and I was doing the same thing, only regular sweat, not blood. The temperature in the dungeon was in the 90s.

The picture of Jesus was a free gift when my parents bought the bed in the corner fifty years earlier from Kash D. Amburgy's Big Bargain Barn furniture store in South Lebanon, Ohio. I laid back on the bed and could still hear Kash's commercial on the TV from when I was a kid. "Just follow the cars, and follow the signs, to Kash's Big Bargain Barn in South Lebanon, Ohio, where you save cash with Kash." I missed being a kid.

The picture of Jesus had always hung in the living room of every place we ever lived in since I was little. I wasn't sure why He had been demoted to the dungeon, maybe to be in there with me. The picture was about a foot wide and a foot and a half in length. The frame was imitation wooden sticks made of plaster material. Over time, two opposite corners had been chipped off. Jesus was looking up toward his Father in heaven.

Breaking a mirror is supposed to be seven years of bad luck, so how many years of bad luck is breaking the corner off the frame of a picture of Jesus worth? I'm sure it's plenty, maybe banishment to the dungeon. I lay there wondering if I had broken it. The Lord's white robe had gotten entirely stained from nicotine with all the cigarette smoking that had gone on in his presence.

On the other hand, the painting of the owl fit perfectly in the dungeon. The owl sat perched on a limb, looking toward his right. The limb seemed dead except for a few air plants growing. Of course, the air plants could have been real; it was an old painting and had been hanging in there for a while. The owl was supposed to be a great horned owl, but this owl had lost its horns. The painting was three-and-a-half-feet square with the ugliest lime-green color I'd ever seen. And, just like with Jesus's, the constant exposure to cigarette smoke had taken its toll. The crappy-looking diarrhea lime green now had a brown hue from the nicotine cast over it. However, it was an original Minoosh, or at least that's who had the guts to sign the painting.

The strange thing about these two paintings is the angle at which they had been hung. The angle I had looking at them from lying on the bed in the dungeon; Jesus and the owl seem to be staring intently at one another. I would sometimes lie there looking at Jesus staring at the owl and the owl staring back at Jesus. I would imagine the conversation they were having. Usually, it was about me, so I naturally had to join in the conversation.

To some, that might sound like blasphemy, but think about it briefly before you damn me to hell. Who was the wisest person ever? Jesus. And, which animal represents wisdom? It's the wise old owl. So, when I had problems and needed some wisdom, and I didn't want to talk to anyone about it, Jesus and the owl and I would talk it out. You might call it crazy; I just called it having church in the dungeon. Sometimes my mom would overhear me and ask, "Who are you talking to in there?" and I would say, "Jesus and the owl." She would always say, "Who?" and I would reply, "Yes." I don't think she ever got the "who" and the owl joke.

Mom had a dog named Baxter. Baxter was a giant Pomeranian, or at least that's what the lady at the vet's office had told her. He was a good-size dog for a Pomeranian, even for a giant one, perhaps twenty-five or thirty pounds, with a long golden coat. The lady at the vet's office was also the same lady that Mom occasionally paid to humiliate Baxter by shaving his coat off now and again. From looking at dog photos, I'd have to agree with the crabby lady at the vet's office. Baxter looked like a giant Pomeranian, except when the grumpy lady shaved off his hair. She always left the hair on his head and tail, and then instead of looking like a giant Pomeranian, Baxter looked like a fox with a water head. Maybe that's why the groomer was so grumpy. She had overheard me telling Mom all the other dogs in the neighborhood would laugh at him.

I don't know if any of you have ever seen the Urban Dictionary online, but here are two of the Urban Dictionary's definitions of a water-head: 1) someone with a skinny body and a huge head, 2) somebody with a big ole head. Well, that described Baxter when his coat was shaved. You could tell Baxter hated it, and he had to feel humiliated to look like a big water-headed fox when deep down inside his heart, he knew he was a giant Pomeranian. I'm sure the other dogs in the neighborhood made fun of him.

Baxter and I never bonded very well when I moved into the dungeon. It wasn't Baxter's fault. Baxter always tried. It was me that resisted. At first, I felt guilty that if I showed Baxter any attention, I would be cheating on my dogs I left at home, Sazarac the wonderdog, my chow and Akita mix, and Rudy the destroyer, the most expensive Yorkie in the world. Mostly I was missing my children and my former life. There would be days when the depression would become so heavy, and Baxter was just a reminder of the life I didn't have anymore.

It wasn't hard not to get attached to Baxter. First, I never could get his name right; sometimes, I called him Baxter, and other times Bastard. The worst was when I called him Buster. Mom hated that since that had been her last boyfriend's name. Buster had returned to Kentucky and been locked up in a mental institution, which ended their relationship. That may have been why my mom called me bubbie to Baxter, like I was his brother or something. It was Mom's way of paying me back for calling her dog Buster and asking her if her boyfriend was still in the nut house.

The second reason it was easy not to get attached to Baxter was his breath. It smelled like eight kinds of ass. Baxter was constantly panting, probably because mom wouldn't turn the A/C below eighty degrees. Of course, eighty degrees would have been a welcomed relief in my part of the house. Baxter would pant so hard when he came into the dungeon to visit that I could smell his breath across the room.

On my first morning of waking up in the dungeon, I was brought out of a deep REM sleep by a horrific smell. At first, as I was trying to gain consciousness, I thought I might have used the bathroom on myself during the night. But the stench was worse than that. Maybe I had been kidnapped during the night and buried in a landfill near the decaying roadkill section. I was sleeping with my face right at the edge of the bed. I slowly opened my eyes to see a big water-headed fox smiling (actually panting) mere inches from my face. It wasn't roadkill at a landfill. It wasn't crap in my drawers. It was Baxter's breath. His breath had penetrated through the Ambien and Darvocet–induced coma and brought me out of my REM sleep. This is where his name Bastard came from when I screamed at him, "Get out of here, you stank-breath Bastard!" (Just a side note here, everyone knows that Elvis died from an overdose of Ambien and Darvocet. The moral of that story is that if Elvis would have had a big water-headed, stank-breath, giant Pomeranian at Graceland for a pet instead of the Memphis Mafia, he might still be alive.)

Baxter fit pretty well in the dungeon. He had a few peculiarities himself. Baxter feared thunder and hid behind Mom's chair when it rained. Also, he was afraid of cigarette lighters, which made me wonder about the containers full of lighters Mom collected. Either Mom had been torturing him with lighters or collecting all the lighters she could find to keep anyone else from torturing Baxter. I found that laying one of the containers of lighters beside the edge of the bed stopped me from being awakened by the smell of eight kinds of ass in my face in the mornings.

Baxter's favorite thing was coming in from being let outside, where he pissed on every inanimate object in the yard. Mom gave him treats for going out to "do his business." But, like everything in the dungeon, there was a frugal and complex order of doing things. Mom bought several types of cheap dog treats for Baxter's reward for "doing his business." There were a certain amount of goodies and a particular type of treat, and this was all determined by what time of day or night it was and which business he did.

Baxter liked it best when I took him out. I couldn't remember the order of the treats, which drove Mom crazy. I would do like I did kids trick-or-treating at Halloween; I'd give him a handful of them all. But just for everyone's sake, if you are wondering about the order of things, here's the way Mom explained it:

"In the morning, he gets one of these unless he pees, then he gets two," she said, pointing at the Alpo Variety Snaps. "In the evening, if he poops, he gets one of these," pointing at the Ol' Roy grilled strips, "and a couple of these," now pointing at the Ol' Roy fake mini T-bone steaks.

I would repeat it to her in a different order on purpose, so she'd go over it again. After she repeated it all once more, I'd say, "That's what I said." She would get mad at me and say, "No, you didn't," and repeat back what I had said, then tell me the proper order again. I would reply, "Oh, okay, now I've got it," and then throw him a handful of Alpo Variety Snaps. Usually, at that point, she would throw up her hands and say, "Whatever!" and storm back into the living room, pick up the TV remote, and turn Judge Joe Brown's volume up to 100%. Baxter loved these discussions. Mom had him on a diet, so I had to learn the proper distribution of treats. He would look back and forth at us, his big water head bobbing from side to side, all grinning and panting with his stank breath, devouring all the treats we were throwing him as examples during these daily discussions.

Alpo Variety Snaps looked like ginger snaps to me, except most were tan, but it had a few dark brown ones thrown in the box to add variety. I don't know if the dark brown tasted any different from the tan ones. I've always heard dogs are color blind, so I don't know if Baxter recognized the variety or if he cared. Mom would have been pissed if she knew how much Baxter loved her Nabisco's Cheez-Its. She always complained that I was eating them. I didn't like them, but Baxter sure did, almost as much as he liked my leftover meatball subs from Subway. I lost a lot of weight during this time, but Baxter packed it on.

Through the months I lived in the Dungeon, Baxter and I finally bonded and reached an agreement. Baxter came to respect my sleep and kept his breath to himself, and I would keep all the cigarette lighters a safe distance from him. During thunderstorms, he would come into the dungeon instead of hiding behind Mom's chair, and I would comfort him with Mom's Cheez-Its.

During one of my dungeon church services, lying there on the bed looking at Jesus and the owl, I began to understand that Baxter had been

Mom's only companion before I moved back there. Baxter gave her a purpose. He was the reason she got out of bed in the morning to let him out to do his business. Baxter was the reason she left the house to buy him food and treats and take him to get his awful grooming. He is the one that heard all the complaints about how no one ever called or came by and visited. He was the one who had to listen to the TV so loud you could hear it in three states, four if the wind was out of the southwest. Something we all learn as we grow old and our children grow up, life can get very lonely, and our pets help to fill that loneliness.

So, Baxter and I formed our own little "dungeon bond," and we each fulfilled our roles. I gave Mom something to complain about by breaking the dog treat rules and pulling pranks. Baxter helped fill that loneliness, and he ate the treats. And like Jesus and the owl said, "Even in the dungeon, a dog is man's best friend." I needed a best friend during that time, and Baxter became mine.

Chapter 8

My Mom—The Warden of the Dungeon and Guardian of the Cigarette Lighters

One of Mom's lighter collections

I say my mom was the warden of the dungeon partly in jest, but it is also true no one could throw a surprise shakedown like my mama could. At almost any time, day or night, I could expect her to walk into my room, rummage through my things, and question me about every item I brought into the dungeon. It started in high school. I kept a journal back then with all my secret thoughts and feelings and what I was doing. Years later, I found out she had kept tabs on me by reading my journal. It initially made me mad, but it paid off in the long run. I already knew her tactics. When I moved back into the dungeon, I kept things I didn't want my Mom to find in a box of stuff my son Caleb had left when he went into the army. I figured I would blame it on my son if she saw anything questionable,

My mom was born during the Great Depression of the 1930s. I've found that many people born and raised during the depression, especially those raised poor tend to be packrats and save everything. Mom had drawers full of many useless items. There were drawers full of buttons, there were drawers full of knobs, and there were drawers full of tubes from old TV sets. When she passed away, I inherited all these useless items, and now I sit and wait for old tube TVs to come back in style. But the most unusual things she kept were old non-working Bic cigarette lighters. She kept them in empty, clear plastic dog treat containers. They were an assortment of colors and designs, and although she was a chain smoker, I have no idea how she collected so many. She thought they looked pretty, all stacked in the dog treat container. I must admit that once, they did come in handy when I couldn't find a lighter. I searched through the containers until I found one with fluid and another with flint. I could hold them close enough to get a flame and light a cigarette. One day, while I was at work, the warden did a shakedown on her empty lighters. When I got home, I was immediately met at the door with the plastic container stuck in my face.

"Have you been messing with these lighters?" Mom asked.

"I used a couple of them last night to light a cigarette."

"They don't work."

"I took one with fluid and one with flint together and made fire."

"How did you learn how to do that?" Mom asked, looking perplexed.

"I was in Cub Scouts and got a fire-making badge."

"Well, put them back in the jar right next time. I had to take them all out and fix them."

Now I had a perplexed look on my face. I had a lot of questions. Did she have them color-coordinated? Had they been sorted by the date she put them in the container? Was there some astrological reasoning behind these lighters, and had she sorted them by the placement of the planets and constellations? I knew to let this sleeping dog lie because I wouldn't understand her explanation anyway. I handed her my empty lighter from the night before and said, "Yes, ma'am, and here's one for your collection for all the trouble I've caused."

I don't know if my mom had been a secret agent or what in her younger years, but if not, she should have been because no one could interrogate like my mom. When she was on the trail for information, she was relentless. The military and police detectives could have taken lessons from her. She had a rapid-fire technique. Any answer you gave would lead to double the questions. These questions would start compounding until I didn't even know what I was answering or why, and before I could figure it out, she'd throw in a totally unrelated question to throw me off.

Anyone who knows me knows I'm not a morning person. I hardly can function until the third pot of coffee. The first thing I want after hitting the snooze button repeatedly for an hour is coffee and silence. The first morning I had to go to work after moving in with my mom, I got dressed and put on my gym shoes instead of my work boots. I went into the kitchen, sat at the table, and started drinking the coffee Mom had poured for me.

Mom asked, "You going to wear those shoes to work?"

"Yep," I said, looking down at my gym shoes, wondering at what point in the snooze alarm I had put them on and whether or not I had socks on underneath them, just in case that was the next question.

"You're not going to wear your work boots?"

"Nope," I said, sipping the coffee and trying to remember if I really needed to work that day.

"I thought you had to wear steel-toed boots out there at the shop."

"It's a phosphate mine, and I do," I replied, trying to figure out why she called every place someone worked at "the shop."

"You're not going to wear yours?"

"Not now," I said, looking at the coffee in the cup, wondering how many more swallows I had before I needed to get up and get a refill and mulling over a list of excuses in my mind I could use to call out of work and go back to bed.

"Why not?"

"Why not what?" I asked.

"Why are you not wearing your boots to the shop?"

"Don't know," I replied, trying to keep my answers to two words or less so I wouldn't get confused by my answers and open the door for more questions. The whole time I'm looking for a fork on the table to jab into my skull.

Mom left the room. I was surprised and relieved that my last answer had halted the interrogation. I reached across the table, took the coffee pot off the table, and started refilling my coffee cup. Suddenly I was startled by a "BAM!" as my work boots hit the floor beside my feet. I missed the cup with the coffee.

"Shit!" I exclaimed, trying to find the paper towels in the clutter on the table to clean up the spilled coffee.

"There's your work boots. What time do you have to be at the shop?"

"It's a phosphate mine, and right now," I said, not knowing what time it was, just knowing I needed to go because she was switching questioning tactics with loud noises to distract me.

Besides an interrogator, she could have been a bombardier in the war because she had dropped those boots from chest high and purposely landed them within an inch of my feet. Now, I either had to pick them up, or put them on, or have to step over them. I still wasn't coherent enough from my Ambien hangover to put them on. There were too many laces to loop and tie and one cup of coffee wasn't enough to do any fancy stepping-over maneuvers. I bent over, picked them up, and started toward my truck outside.

"You're not going to put them on?"

"I'll put them on when I get to work," I said, not wanting to go into detail that I had two other pairs of work boots I kept in my work truck at "the shop," especially since she had gone to all the trouble to get the pair she dropped at my feet.

"You're not going to take any coffee with you?" Mom asked as I was heading out the door to the truck.

"I don't have a cup to put it in."

"Here's the one you've been drinking from."

"It doesn't have a cover, and I'll spill it on the rough road into the mine."

"Well, wait a minute. I'll be right back," Mom said as she ran back into the house, still in her bed jacket and Walmart house shoes.

I could already tell, as I threw the work boots in the bed of my pickup truck, that one – and two-word answers wouldn't work at the dungeon. I would have to learn to assemble entire sentences early in the morning or wake up earlier to avoid questioning. I knew waking up earlier wouldn't happen, so complete sentences would have to be constructed. I cranked up my truck and was about to back out of the yard when I saw Mom coming back out of the house.

"Here, this won't spill," Mom said, handing me a McDonald's drink cup with a cheap plastic lid and a straw.

"Thanks, I love you," I said, taking the cup and putting the truck in gear.

"I love you too," she said, kissing me on the cheek. "Don't forget your boots in the back of the truck when you get to the shop."

"I won't, and it's not a shop; it's a phosphate mine," I said out the window as I drove off.

She didn't have to tell me she loved me. I knew she did. Why else would anyone run back in the house and wash out an old McDonald's cup, complete with a cheap plastic lid and a straw? I drove along, sipping on the coffee and looking at the cup, thinking a mother's love is about as close as you can get to the love of Jesus. They love you despite yourself or whether you're deserving or not. They love and nurture you no matter how old you become. I knew my life was changing, and living in the dungeon would be much different and adventurous. But still, to this day, I haven't figured out how she knew I had taken those two lighters out of the container. That's something else mothers and Jesus have in common. They just know things.

Chapter 9

The Rain Gauge and the Payback

LIVINGSTON INN MOTEL

Emily Seelinger
Andy Carter

Interstate 90
Exit 333
#5 Rogers Lane
Livingston, MT 59047
(406) 222-3600
livingstoninn@montana.net
www.livingstoninnmotel.com

One hot summer Florida evening, after living in the dungeon a few months, we had a bad thunderstorm, and lightning knocked out several transformers. The power was out for quite a while. The rain had cooled it off a little, so I went to bed at about 10:30 p.m. that night. It reminded me of those good old Hurricane Charley nights without air conditioning. I opened the window, but there wasn't any breeze, just stifling humidity, and I couldn't even run a fan because of no power. Finally, at about two in the morning, I couldn't take the heat and sweat anymore and had to go outside. I walked around the yard, trying to decide whether to scream at the top of my lungs, "Two o'clock, and all's well!" I knew Mom was too hard of hearing to hear me, and I could hear her snoring through her bedroom window. I sat on the front porch and lit a cigarette. That's when I spied Mom's rain gauge I had put up for her a few weeks earlier.

The rain gauge had been a source of contention between Mom and me since I had attached it to the post. She'd come home with a cheap $2 rain gauge from Walmart one day and wanted me to put it on her dinner bell post. I had taken the bell down a year earlier because little hoodlums would sneak and ring it. I wanted to put an electric wire to the bell to give them a little shock for their trouble, but Mom was against that, so I took the bell down and just left the post in the middle of the front yard. She wouldn't let me remove the post. She probably wanted one more obstacle to mow around, or she already had a rain gauge planned in her future.

The post was four inches by four inches square and stood seven feet high in the air. I told her I needed to cut the post down some to put the rain gauge on top, or she wouldn't be able to see it, let alone reach it to dump the rain out. But she insisted I mount the rain gauge on the side of the post. I argued that the post would block some of the rain. It wouldn't be accurate. After about five minutes of arguing about the physics of rainfall, I just gave up and mounted the dang thing on the side like she wanted. I figured out she didn't care about how accurate it was. The sole purpose of the rain gauge was to give her sister, my aunt Gwen, in Kentucky, daily weather report from Florida.

My aunt and mom would call each other several times a day and give each other weather reports and discuss the latest family gossip. When long-distance phone service became free, they would watch TV game shows for hours together on the phone. Mom used to stay the summers with my aunt Gwen in Livingston, Kentucky. The best way to describe my Mom and Aunt is they were like the "Baldwin" sisters from the old Walton TV series or the Thelma and Louise movie. When school was out, my mom would go to Kentucky to stay a few months with her sister. One summer evening, I got a call from my mom.

"Guess where I'm at?"

"At Aunt Gwen's or the nut house with Buster?" I asked.

"No, smart aleck. I'm in Livingston, alright, but not Kentucky. We're in Livingston. Montana!" Mom said, all excited.

"Why?"

"Well, we were sitting at Gwen's looking at the Rand McNally Road Atlas, and we saw a Livingston, Montana, packed our bags, and drove two days to get here. We got a nice room for fifty dollars. The man wanted ninety for the room, but Gwen told him she only had fifty dollars cash. Then he tried to charge us tax, but Gwen said all she had was fifty. So we got the room for the night for fifty dollars, tax and all. And we get a free breakfast in the morning."

"Well, aren't you two just a couple of wild and crazy gals? What are you going to do there?"

"Nothing, we just drove up to take a picture of the Livingston, Montana city limits sign. We're heading back to Kentucky after our free breakfast in the morning."

"How are you all getting back if all you have is fifty dollars?"

"We've got money. We weren't going to pay ninety dollars for a room. I'll call you when we get back to Kentucky. I love you."

"I love you too. I'm calling the Livingston Montana Police Department when we hang up and reporting you two for room tax evasion," I said, laughing, still shaking my head.

"You better not, you little *idget*. Bye."

That was my mom and my aunt Gwen in a nutshell.

Now back to the story after that Mom and Aunt Gwen newsbreak. So there I am, at two in the morning, sitting on my Mom's front porch in the humidity and the darkness, looking at a seven-foot-tall post standing alone in the middle of the yard. I checked the rain gauge to get a rough estimate of how much rain we had received. I pulled the gauge out of the bracket and held it up to the moon, which was breaking through the clouds. With all that thunder and lightning and power outage, we had only gotten a mere half an inch of rain. My mom would surely be disappointed during her morning weather report call to my aunt. My aunt in Kentucky could spit more than half an inch of rain. I could tell by the sound of her snoring coming from her bedroom window beside the porch that she was dreaming of a full rain gauge. I couldn't let Mom be disappointed.

That's when I saw the cat's water dish on the porch. An idea occurred in my head, and try as I might, I couldn't resist. I knew how thrilled my mom would be in the morning when she called in her Florida rain report. I filled the rain gauge with five inches of the cat's water for a grand total of five and a half inches. Soon the power came back on, and I went back into the dungeon to sleep. I turned the window AC unit I had saved up and bought as cold as it would cool.

That morning, I was sleepily brushing my teeth at the kitchen sink, getting ready for work after only three hours of sleep from the night before. I had forgotten all about the rain gauge. I was in mid-stroke with the toothbrush when a glass rain gauge with five and a half inches of water appeared in front of my face. At first, I wasn't sure what it was, and then I heard Mom exclaim, "Lookie, five and a half inches!" I spit toothpaste all over the place, belly laughing when I remembered what I had done.

"What are you laughing about?" Mom asked.

"It didn't rain that much."

"Yes, it did. Look!" Mom said, excited and wanting to call her sister at 6:30 in the morning. She wiped some of the toothpaste I'd spit on the side of the rain gauge and pointed at the five-and-a-half-inch mark.

"I put that in there."

"No, you didn't."

"Yes, I did," I said, laughing and spitting the toothpaste out.

"When?"

"About two this morning when I went outside because my room was too hot to sleep."

"You're an asshole!" Mom said as she turned and stormed out of the kitchen to put her rain gauge back in the holder now that her rainfall bragging rights to my aunt had been crushed.

I was still trying to finish getting ready for work when she came back inside, and I could hear her in the living room talking to her dog, Baxter the Waterhead. "Your Bubbie's an asshole. He's mean."

Baxter didn't care. As long as I gave him a couple of extra dog treats, he still loved me.

"You going to the nut doctor today?" Mom asked as she walked back into the kitchen.

"Yeah, this afternoon."

"Ain't no use in you going to the doctor," talking about my mental health therapist.

"Why?"

"Cause you're too mean. The doctor can't do you no good."

"Huh?" I asked, still trying to figure out today what that meant.

"You going to work now?" Mom started with her rapid-fire questions as I was going out the door.

"I'm not sure I can get there this morning."

"Why?"

"The river bridge may be under water after five and a half inches of rain," I said, laughing, walking out the door to get in my truck.

"You're still an asshole!" she said again as she slammed the door behind me. I could hear her telling Baxter how mean "Bubbie" was and that no nut doctor could help me.

Every dog's Bubbie has its day, and a few weeks later I had mine. Mom paid me back. As I got to work, I walked down the hall in my office building and felt a strong breeze blowing on my right butt cheek. I didn't get the nickname Commando Rando for my acts of heroism in battle. No, I got it because I usually dress Commando. I don't like to wear underwear. This particular morning, I was getting a strong southerly draft from the rear end of my britches. I quickly entered the men's room to check out what was happening. I pulled my pants down to find the whole right side of the rear end of my pants ripped open.

An iron-on patch that had been put inside my britches had let go somewhere in my travels that morning. I recognized the jeans as the pair I had thrown in the trash several weeks earlier. I'm not a morning person, so in my morning stupor of running late and trying to get dressed and drink coffee simultaneously, I'd grabbed the first clean pair of jeans I could find and hadn't paid any attention to the patching work.

I've written in earlier chapters how Mama hates to throw anything away. I had ripped the rear end out of these pants weeks earlier crossing through a barbwire fence and had thrown them in the trash at Mom's. She had dug them out of the garbage and put an iron-on patch on them. I didn't even know they still made iron patches, so she must have had this one from the 1960s, which would explain why it hadn't bonded to my pants.

I pulled my shirt out, looked up and down the hall, and made a bee-line for my truck before anyone saw me. I called my friend Bill, whom I was supposed to meet at the office and go out and sample a creek with that morning. I explained my dilemma and told him to meet me at a convenience store near our workplace. Luckily for me, this convenience store sold used pants that were cleaned up and packaged to sell to the migrant workers that worked the agricultural fields in this area. You could never trust the sizes on the packages, so I had to buy three pairs just to be safe that one pair would fit me.

I stood holding my shirt down, covering my exposed behind, waiting for the store owner to ring up the used pants, half listening to him telling me how many of those pants he sells and half listening to Bill standing behind me laughing, all the while cussing under my breath wondering why my mother would dig a pair of ripped jeans out of the garbage and put a cheap forty-year-old iron-on patch on them and not say anything. Finally, Bill and I got to the woods, and I immediately stripped out of the ripped jeans and put on the used fruit-picking pants. I walked out from behind my truck and asked Bill, "Do you think these pants make me look fat?" He was still laughing. I threw the ripped ones in the back of my work truck and later in the dumpster at work, far, far, away where Mom would never find them again.

When I got home from work, I told Mom about the pants.

"What did you do with them?" she asked.

"I threw them in the dumpster at the office."

"You should have brought them back."

"Why?" I asked, "So you could try and patch them again?"

"No, so you could wear them the next time we get five and a half inches rain. You can dump the water out of the hind end while you're wading across the river bridge."

I looked at Baxter, sitting by my mom, who seemed to be grinning at me, and said, "Our momma is mean, Baxter."

Mom started laughing and reached for the phone to call her co-conspirator in Kentucky and tell her that their plan had worked liked a charm.

Chapter 10

The Fingernail Clipper Caper

I learned from experience while living in the dungeon that if I couldn't find something, I shouldn't say anything and just look for it myself. If I did say anything, God bless my momma's sweet heart, she was on the way full steam ahead, and the hunt was on. It didn't matter what she was doing. Once, she was using the toilet, and I asked out loud, "Have you seen my keys?" The toilet immediately flushed, and she busted open the door, still pulling at her clothes. She was in the hunt like a hound dog on a trail, except she didn't run her own trail. She followed mine. Wherever I would look, she'd be right there next to me, looking in the same place, like two kids looking for Easter eggs. Mom was that one kid that always tries to grab the egg first. Then, if she found the lost object first, she would call my aunt Gwen in Kentucky, just like with the rain gauge. She would declare herself the winner and tell her sister every detail of the hunt.

While looking for the keys, as soon as I would move an item to look behind it, her hand would be right there, ready to snatch the first shiny item that remotely looked like a set of keys. I'd sigh, shake my head, and say, "You know if we split up, we can cover more ground."

"Well, where did you have them last?" Mom would ask.

"The last time I remember having them was in my truck."

Boom! There she went as fast as she could out the back door and headed to my truck, still in her nightgown and housecoat, her flattened house shoes flopping all the way to the truck. After a few minutes, Mom would come in and say, "They're not in your truck!"

"I know that. I've already looked."

"You could have told me that before I went out there!"

"I could have, but I needed some alone time so I could find my keys," I said, holding up my truck keys and jingling them at her.

"Next time, you can find them yourself."

"That's what I just did."

"Whatever, as if. You can kiss my foot. Come on, Baxter, your Bubbie is full of foolishness," Mom said, returning to the living room and turning the TV up full blast.

One day I was in the dungeon looking for fingernail clippers, and before I thought I asked Mom (who was in the kitchen), "Have you seen my clippers?" As soon as the words left my mouth, I thought, "Oh crap," to myself. Mom came busting into the dungeon with Baxter in tow, scanning the horizon, trying to get a hit on the fingernail clipper trail.

"What?" she asked.

"Never mind," I replied, relieved she didn't hear me and thinking it was a close call.

"What clippers? Fingernail clippers? Where'd you have them?"

Once again, Mom was using her rapid-fire questioning technique, so I knew she meant business. She was like a machine gun of questions. Bam! Bam! Bam! One after the next. One minute I'm like a soldier walking along a jungle trail looking for booby traps. The next minute, I'm hit with an explosion of questions, and before I can answer, I've been hit with the second and then the third. Soon, I would find myself with the life draining from me as I tried to answer something from four questions ago. I just stood there thinking to myself, "Why did I have to talk out loud? I just wanted some fingernail clippers to get rid of a hangnail."

One of life's greatest mysteries to me was Mom's hearing. She couldn't hear the space shuttle if it were blasting off in the front yard, but talk out loud to yourself, wondering where something was. Boom! She hears every word, and even though she may say, "What?" it's always followed up by naming whatever you are looking for and then, "Where'd you have them?"

"Yes, fingernail clippers, and if I knew where I had them, I'd go get them!" I replied while I moved things on the table in the backroom next to my door leading into the dungeon, looking for the clippers.

"Maybe I left them in the truck," I said, hoping it would work again.

"I'm not as stupid as you look," Mom replied, tapping me up beside the head for trying to trick her again.

Mom was now in hot pursuit and standing within an inch of my right side, hovering. She was waiting for me to move something to reveal the fingernail clipper so she could snatch them before I could. When I reached to look behind something, she would grab it before I could and move it, hoping to find the Easter egg disguised as fingernail clippers. If Mom did, she would declare herself the winner, and then Aunt Gwen would get a call immediately detailing the whole story, especially since it hadn't rained lately.

Finally, I stepped back, sighed deeply, and said again, "I think if we split up, we can cover more ground." Then it occurred to me that the last time I saw them, they were on the dresser in the dungeon. I opened the door and closed it behind me, leaving Mom still searching on the table in the next room. As I looked on top of the dresser, I glanced down and saw something metallic on the floor behind it. I pulled the dresser out a little; low and behold; there were the clippers.

I felt relieved that the search could now be called off. The hound could stand down. I could hear Mom still ravaging across the table in the next room in hot pursuit of the clippers. As I bent over to pick them up, I said, "I found them!" That, again, was a mistake.

About the time I bent down to reach and grab the clippers and my head was doorknob high, Mom slammed open the door, trying to beat me to them. The doorknob hit me squarely in the head above my right ear. After the door knob slammed into the right side of my head, due to the physic's law of the transference of energy, the left side of my head slammed into the dresser just as my fingers were almost close enough to touch the clippers. The double jar to my head caused me to touch the clippers just enough with my outstretched fingers to send them flying under the far side of the dresser. It was like a hockey player finessing a puck into the goal but I felt like a pinball that just got popped with both flippers. I just sat back with my knees up, holding both sides of my head in disbelief.

"Where they at?" she asked.

At this point, I had given up. I didn't even remember I had a hang-nail. I just nodded toward the dresser and mumbled, "Under there."

I didn't even have to look up. I could feel Mom's excitement as she realized she would get the prize egg. Suddenly, instead of letting me recover from my double concussion for a moment and help her, Mom grabbed the corner of the dresser and gave it a jerk with all her might. The corner of the dresser slammed into my still-raised left knee. Fortunately, it was, or at least had been, my good knee. The pain that shot through my knee made me forget for a moment about the goose egg that was beginning to form over my right ear. Before the pain from my knee could mingle with the pain from both sides of my head to form one giant throb, Mom stepped on my ankle, reaching down to pick up the clippers. My bad right ankle. The one which had been broken in three places playing baseball.

"Here they are!" she proudly proclaimed, flipping them towards me and hitting me right in the forehead. "You ought to keep them in that bowl over there so they won't fall behind the dresser," she said, as she stepped back onto my ankle again and out the door.

"Okay. Tell Aunt Gwen I love her, and I should be alright in a month or two," I said, still sitting there on the floor senseless, looking up at the pictures of the wise old owl and Jesus praying in the garden, hanging there on the wall above me, while shaking my head in disbelief.

I sat there for a minute and took a deep breath, trying to gather my thoughts, looking first at the picture of the owl on my right, then to the picture of Jesus on my left. Finally, I mumbled, "Why?"

"Forgive her; she knows not what she does," Jesus said.

The owl didn't know what to say after watching a grown man get a beat down by his eighty-year-old mother over a pair of fingernail clippers. The owl just rolled its eyes and said, "Whatever, as if." Mom's favorite phrase when she didn't know what else to say.

Chapter 11

Leaving the Dungeon

Rudy and me at the Bartow Apartment, Christmas 2009

I lived in Momma's dungeon for six months or so. In the beginning, I saw my mental health therapist, whom Mom called my "nut doctor," several times a week. I never told Mom what was discussed or about the suicide incident at the beach bungalow. I never told anyone except Dorothy, my therapist. Dorothy kept me on a writing regime during this time, which is where all these stories come from.

There were still bouts of depression, but I would write through it. It was as much a part of my therapy as my sessions with Dorothy were.

I would write every night. Sometimes just thoughts and feelings, some-times short stories, and of course these stories about Mom and living in the dungeon.

People loved the stories about Mom and she became a semi-celebrity on Myspace. She would get Christmas cards from people from around the country that she didn't know. She acted like she didn't care, but I knew she loved it. I was never making fun of my mom. I was chronicling our lives as total opposites living in a small house. I would sometimes hear her on the speakerphone with my aunt Gwen telling her about some of her cards. They always talked on speakerphone because they were both hard of hearing.

Mom would tell Aunt Gwen, "I got a Christmas card from someone in Nevada."

"Who was it?" Aunt Gwen would ask.

"I don't know. Somebody who reads that foolishness Randall writes about us." (Mom always called me Randall, never Randy.)

"Well, he's making you famous. Tell him to write one about me. I want some Christmas cards," Aunt Gwen would laugh and say.

"I think he's about crazy. He has to go and see that 'nut doctor' all the time."

Mom never realized how loudly she talked because of her hearing, but Baxter and I could hear every word.

Things began to change for the better for me. Thinking Stephanie and my relationship was over; I started seeing a much younger woman named Kristin. I finally received a promotion at work to environmental supervisor. I had been passed over for the position many times before. With the promotion came quite a bit of a raise in salary. I could finally start looking for a place of my own to live.

The writing had kept the depression at bay, and I hadn't had suicidal thoughts since that weekend at the beach. My visits to the therapist had been cut back from several times a week to once every couple of weeks. I talked about moving out of the dungeon with my therapist, and she too thought it was time. I found an old, small duplex of a place about twenty miles north in the town of Bartow, Florida.

Leaving the dungeon was as emotional as moving into it had been. It was very tearful the day I packed up. My mom and I had become accustomed to the organized chaos we had brought to one another's lives. I think Baxter the Waterhead was the saddest. When I left, I gave him a whole handful of treats to keep him occupied so he didn't have to see me go.

I moved to the historic district of Bartow. The duplex I moved into had a lot of history but was far from historical. I lived around the block from where the movie *My Girl* was made and up the street from where *China Moon* had been filmed.

Although I was occasionally dating Kristin, Stephanie would come and see me. We would spend time together and sit and talk, and sometimes go out to eat. We decided to try to fix our marriage one last time. I told Kristin that Stephanie and I were going to try and fix our marriage, and I couldn't see her anymore.

Besides me seeing my own therapist, Stephanie and I saw a marriage counselor. Finally, after one session, the marriage counselor told us both, "I have no idea how you two got together to begin with, but my suggestion to you both is to get as far away from one another as possible." It was what we both already knew, but we did try. We left the therapist's office, went bowling together, and laughed about what he had said. We worked out an agreement between us. We had dinner at a Mexican restaurant in Bartow. I still didn't want a divorce but I reluctantly signed the divorce papers. It wasn't always easy through the years, but we always put our children first and remained friends, as I have with all my former wives.

As part of the agreement, I kept my little retirement in my 401k, and she also gave me Rudy, the most expensive Yorkie in the world. I would take Rudy for a walk around the neighborhood in the evenings. Without fail, he would stop right in front of the Stanford Inn, where *My Girl* was filmed. On the exact spot where Jamie Lee Curtis stepped off the RV onto the sidewalk, Rudy would go crazy and sniff all around like she was just there. Then he would go to where Macaulay Culkin and Dan Aykroyd once stood and peed. I don't know the significance of Rudy doing that. It's anyone's guess, but I supposed he was like me and liked Jamie Lee better than the other two. I can't watch that movie anymore because it's too sad. Not that the film is sad, although it is a tear-jerker of a movie, the memories of Rudy make me sad. During this time, Rudy was to me what Baxter had been to my mom. He gave me company during the loneliness and he gave me purpose.

The duplex I moved into was old and wooden with no insulation. It had been built in the 1920s, or so I guessed. It had high ceilings, which held the heat in the summer, and was nearly as hot as the dungeon. It was also impossible to heat on the few cold days we had in the winter. I would boil water on the stove to provide extra warmth until the condensation would build up on the ceiling and drop like little raindrops inside the house.

Once, a friend from work named Kevin Dooley dropped by to check out my new place. The first thing out of his mouth was, "Man, I hope you're not paying too much for this dump?"

I replied, "I'm sorry, Kevin, it doesn't have wheels like your house." Kevin lived in a mobile home.

The place did have a few amenities the dungeon hadn't provided. First, I had privacy, but sometimes that meant loneliness. There was enough room where my younger kids could spend the weekends. And it had a lovely, enclosed front porch that was perfect to sit on and write. An elderly lady lived across the old oak-lined street. When the weather was nice, she would open her windows and play the piano beautifully. It provided an excellent ambiance for sitting out there on the porch and writing.

Nighttime was the worst there. It was just me and Rudy most of the time. I would be alone with my thoughts and memories. I missed my old life. I missed my kids. And I even missed the dungeon with my mom and Baxter. My writing began to escape me. To keep my mind occupied and not allow the depression to get another foothold, I started going online and playing with my 401K account from my job.

I had no idea what I was doing, but I could never afford to contribute to it because I was always trying to get by to provide for my family. The only money I had in the 401k was what my company had invested for me. And now, I had very little money left over every week after I paid my alimony, child support, and bills, and I still couldn't contribute. One night I thought, "What the heck, I've got nothing to lose but the little bit the company had invested," so I started buying and selling stocks within my 401K account.

Call it beginners luck or the Lord's guidance. I think it was God because I don't believe in luck. Soon I had tripled the money in my 401k without knowing what I was doing buying and selling stocks. I had enough money to get my 110-year-old house out of foreclosure and bankruptcy. Stephanie agreed to allow me to have full ownership of the old house, and my oldest son, Randy, who was now an attorney, helped me with all the paperwork to get the old house back.

The old house was in terrible disrepair. It had been sitting abandoned for over a year. It had received damage from hurricanes. It had been vandalized, had holes in the floors, walls, and ceiling, and was basically uninhabitable. After I owed the house outright, I took the money I had left over from borrowing from my 401k to get it and I began working evenings and weekends to make one room fit to live in.

During this time, I had almost stopped writing altogether. I stayed too busy working. I had stopped playing with my 401k because the company changed the investment rules, and I couldn't flip stock like I had been doing when I made all the money. Except for occasional depression and darkness, I stayed too busy with my job and working on the house to allow it to suck me back in.

Finally, Rudy and I packed our belongings, left the dump without wheels, and moved back to Bowling Green. Kristin and I had been seeing each other for over a year and had become serious, and she moved in with me. One evening in mid-December, we began discussing marriage while she watched as I worked repairing a hole in the floor on the front porch.

It was here that I made the most romantic marriage proposal in the history of mankind. While on my knees in the hole and amongst broken boards and wood rot, I said, "Well if we are going to get married, we need to do it before the end of the year. That way, we can file married/filing jointly, or else I will have to pay a crap load of taxes this year."

She agreed to marry me. How could she not with such a romantic proposal made by a man on his knees in a hole in a front porch, right smack dab in the middle of downtown Bowling Green, Florida—to a man who already had the forethought to be thinking about the upcoming tax year?

I immediately called my close friend Pam Williams, whom I worked with, and who was also a notary public. Pam was on vacation at the time and was in the middle of a massage at a spa when I called. She asked if I could call her later. I said no. I needed her to marry me before the end of the year. She replied, between her moaning and groaning from her massage, "I'm flattered, Randy, but I can't. I'm already married."

I explained the situation, and she said she could do it at her house on December 28. Thinking back, my implied proposal to my friend Pam was more romantic than my actual proposal to Kristin. Still, Kristin and I were married at my friend's home on December 28, 2010.

It was my third marriage. Kristin was finishing nursing school. She was twenty-six years younger than me and had graduated high school with my third-oldest son, Caleb. With such a romantic marriage proposal and with such an age difference, what could go wrong? It seemed like a marriage made in heaven and quite beneficial, tax-wise.

Once again, things seemed to be changing for the better for me. I continued to see my therapist, but only monthly now. I rarely suffered from the darkness and depression that had driven me to consider suicide. Over the next five years, all that seemed like a distant nightmare. Kristin graduated and began working as an RN. I was making good money and had paid off all my debts. I lived close to most of my kids. Everyone was getting along. I finally felt hope.

Section Three
My Journey into the Fog

State Road 674, where I first journeyed into the fog

Chapter 12

The Bureaucracy

As mentioned in the previous chapter, things finally started going my way. I worked my way out of debt. I was doing well with my new position at my job. My children began having more children. At the time I had seven grandchildren and more on the way. Life was good. I seldom dealt with the depression. I never thought of suicide, and my therapist said it was okay to stop our sessions. I rarely had time to write and wrote very little, although the stories were always in my mind. And then, the fog started rolling in.

One day at work, I left the office to meet and train one of the guys who worked on my crew. The location was about twenty miles away. I drove along State Road 674, which I had driven several times daily over the previous thirty years. I knew the road like the back of my hand. As I left Polk County, I saw the sign that read "Hillsborough County," and a sudden panic hit me. I didn't know where I was. I didn't know where I was going. And I didn't understand why I was going.

I would drive five or six miles to the Ft. Lonesome Grocery, where I would turn around and return to the Polk/Hillsborough County line, then turn around and do it again. The Ft. Lonesome Grocery store, where I had stopped almost every morning for years, looked familiar, but I still didn't know where I was. I had gone into a total brain fog. Finally, on one of the flip/flop trips, I saw Mike, the guy on my crew I was supposed to be meeting, driving the opposite way, and it was like a switch flipped, and everything returned to me.

I didn't say anything about it. I just tried to put it out of my mind and joked to myself that it was just a flashback to a bad hallucinogenic mushroom trip in the 1970s. Then, it happened several more times. Once, I was on my way home from work, and the same thing happened. I drove back and forth on the road that ran by my house and couldn't remember where I lived. Kristin could tell I was quite flustered when I arrived home. She asked what had happened, and I explained the whole story to her. She called and made me a doctor's appointment. I went to my doctor the next day and explained to the doctor what had been going on. My primary physician immediately took me out of work, and my company put me on short-term disability. I started doing what I always have done when faced with problems: I began to write about my journey into the fog. I began to chronicle my experiences. The following in italics is from one of those writings from that time. Other than just a few small edits, it's basically the same as when I wrote it at the time. You can see a subtle change in my writing as I dealt with the confusion from my memory.

One of the worst things for me with dementia is getting lost. I know many people who wander around aimlessly all day and don't have dementia. But there's a difference between wandering and getting lost. The lost I'm speaking of is terrifying. You do not know where you're at, or how you got to where you are at, or where you're going. You are LOST!

I got lost on my way to my doctor's appointment. I explained to my doctor that I was late for my appointment because I got lost on my way to his office. I told the doctor it was becoming a common occurrence, and I'd been hiding it from everyone. He had been my primary physician for a long time, all the way back through the years of depression. He became more concerned and aggressive with his testing and treatment of my brain's cognitive disorder. What the doctor thought may have been a mild mini-stroke a year earlier led to him thinking I might have mild cognitive disorder. All the tests proved this to be true. Getting lost was one of the changes in my behavior that took me from mild cognitive disorder to dementia. I have a family history of dementia and Alzheimer's disease. But those family members had been much older than me. None had been fifty-six years old when they began to decline.

I had to hand it to my primary physician; he tried everything to keep from diagnosing me with dementia. He sent me here and there, took me off these medications, put me on that medication, and then took me off all medications to see if that was causing my issues. He even sent me to a mental health therapist to ensure it wasn't stress or depression. He sent me to neurologists. All the other doctors and therapists agreed it was dementia. Finally, the neurologist sent me to the University of South Florida, where I was tested for early-onset Alzheimer's.

One of my saddest days was when, after he received all the test results, my primary physician told me I had dementia. According to the doctor who had examined me at the USF, I had early-onset Alzheimer's. I was sad for me and my doctor, who was in tears. He and I had become friends through the years. He was old school. He wasn't one to rush you in and out or one to write you a script to make you feel like he had done his job. He spent time with you, made you feel like you mattered and like he cared. He did care, and more importantly, he listened to his patients. As we sat in his office and he told me I had dementia, with tears in his eyes, he kept telling me, "You're too young for this . . . this is so sad . . . I'm so sorry," repeatedly. I almost cried because he was so upset and started to ask, "Do you want my therapist's card? I think she can help you work through this." I finally patted him on his shoulder and said, "It's alright, Doc, we'll make it through this."

We lived in Kentucky with my maternal grandparents when I was eight and nine. Grandma had suffered a stroke and developed dementia. Mom, my youngest brother, and I moved there so Mom could care for my grandma. My dad stayed in Ohio and would drive down to visit when his work schedule allowed. Grandma was confined to a wheelchair from the stroke and was in the latter stages of dementia. I remember how terrifying it was at that age when she would suffer from hallucinations. Sometimes, imagining hogs were in her bed, she would beat the bed with a broom. Other times, she would start talking to someone she had known years ago, who had long since died, as if they were in the room with her, or she would speak to someone out the window. I would look out the window, and it would just be a bucket hanging upside down on a fence post to keep the water out. I thought to myself, I don't want my grandchildren to see me like that.

Grandma was probably in stage seven. The doctors all suspected from my cognitive tests I was in stage three. Typically, stage three will last about seven years, then it begins to progress faster, and each stage after that goes rather quickly until you reach stage seven. Once in stage seven, the process can slow down again, but the person needs 24/7 caregiving and support at that stage. I wasn't sure how long I'd been in this stage because I kept it hidden for a while.

Many organizations, websites, etc. determine the stages differently, but they are all similar. For simplicity's sake, the following are hospice guidelines.

The symptoms for stage three are the following:

- *Forgetfulness and memory loss (This is similar but more intense than normal aging forgetfulness and memory loss.)*
- *Repetition (Repeating the same story several times)*
- *Losing articles without being able to retrace steps to find them (Again, more severe than not being able to find my car keys and eyeglasses)*
- *Slight trouble managing finances, such as balancing a checkbook and paying bills on time*
- *Confusion while driving*
- *Trouble managing medications*
- *Loss of concentration*

Now, why did I hide it for so long? The simple answer is I didn't realize that was what was wrong. I was only fifty-six years old.

On my way home from the doctor giving the results of the tests, I decided to do what I always did when I didn't know what else to do: to write about what I was going through. I would attempt to chronicle this disease for as long as I had the cognitive ability to write. I hoped to break some of the stigmatisms and myths people have toward dementia and to give loved ones and caregivers a little hope. I somehow hoped to bring enough awareness to the disease to shift the research and testing into high gear. You would think as a country, we would try to devote as many resources to finding a cure for dementia and Alzheimer's instead of wasting money on so many asinine projects that benefit only small special interest groups.

One out of every two people who live to age eighty-five will suffer from some form of dementia, and those who don't will have to take care of those who do. I hoped they would jump on this before it was too late for me. I guess everyone diagnosed with a fatal, incurable disease feels that way. It wasn't my fault I was an early bloomer. Unfortunately, I soon learned that except for those who love and care about you, you don't matter to the politicians, and especially to the insurance companies. Once you are no longer a productive member of society, your life doesn't matter, and to the government and insurance companies, you're cheaper dead than alive.

I was now not allowed to work and went on short-term disability. I would receive 100% of my pay for six months. After six months, I would go on to long-term disability and receive 70% of my salary but would have to buy my insurance through Cobra. Everything was fine during those first six months. I had an excellent, caring human resource representative at my job named Nikki. Nikki would do her best to help me whenever I had an issue. The problems came after my six-month short-term disability ended and the long-term disability began.

I no longer had Nikki as an advocate, and I had to deal with the insurance company directly. At this time, I learned that to a large insurance corporation, it was more profitable for me to die than to live. I had paid for long-term disability, through my paycheck at work, for many years, and when it came time to issue a claim, I found out how worthless it was. I was at my weakest and now would have to fight giants. Some days, I would get lost just going through the telephone prompts to try and reach a live person and have to hang up and start all over again. I think that's part of their strategy to get a person to give up, but I've never been a quitter.

The insurance company contracted a subsidiary company that would help me file for social security disability. I had to fill out a mountain of paperwork, then the subsidiary company kept claiming I was going blind. This happened numerous times. I was finally able to get it through their heads I wasn't going blind; I had been diagnosed with dementia. I supposed it was easier for them to claim blindness than dementia. The subsidiary company told me that I could expect my application for social security disability to be declined three times. After that, I would be appointed a hearing with a judge to decide my fate. If I won, I would be awarded a monthly income and insurance. My insurance company would then make up the balance if the award were less than 70% of my prior salary. If I lost, I was just out of luck except for a lengthy appeal process. It was one level of corrupt bureaucracy after another to deal with, from the politicians to the insurance companies.

Throughout all this time, the neurologist was adjusting my medications. He would schedule me for brain scans every time my insurance company would not approve them. I would file appeal after appeal, but my insurance company would still decline them. The neurologist prescribed Memantine and Aricept for dementia, anti-depressants, and various anxiety medicines. I felt like a zombie. It was easier and cheaper to medicate me than to fix me.

I continued to take Memantine and Aricept for dementia but substituted the rest with a small amount of marijuana. At this time, medical marijuana had not been legalized by Florida. What a world of difference marijuana made instead of the anti-depressants and anxiety medications. I would still have good and bad days, but now, on the good days, I didn't walk around like I was in an episode of *Night of the Living Dead*. On the days I wasn't in a dementia fog, with the marijuana, I could finally write again. I'm a very strong advocate for medical marijuana. But of course anytime there's big money involved, there is greed and corruption. Whether it's illegal with the drug cartels, or legal with the government bureaucracy, the love of money is the root of all evil. During all this time, the depression and darkness kept trying to slip back in, but once again, on the days I could focus, I began to do as I had during the dungeon days: I outwrote the devil.

While I was going through this, unbeknownst to us all, my Mom was also developing dementia. She and I were almost on the same level. I lived across town from my mom, and she often came over daily to visit and check on me. Our conversations on the front porch led to more stories like I had written in the dungeon. I called them Deep Conversations with Momma. All the stories in this section are from this period of my life as I journeyed deeper into the fog.

Chapter 13

Same Sex Marriage and My Mom

Mom sitting on my front porch during one of her daily visits

My mom always had a daily routine. She slept until noon or a little later every day. After getting up and stirring around, Mom would head to the post office and check her mail. Afterward, she drove down Main Street to the town's only red light at US 17. She'd cross Highway 17 to the Dollar General store. I only lived one block west of the Dollar General on Main Street, so she would head to my house after buying her pack of cigarettes. I was happy she slept late because so did I, since I wasn't working anymore.

On this particular day, my pickup truck was parked behind my house. Mom always looked for my truck in the front to make sure I was home before she would stop, even though she would call me on the phone to see if I was home before she left her house. I figured she wanted to be double sure I was home before she traveled those extra five hundred feet from the Dollar General to my home. I decided to wait out on the front porch and drink coffee so she could see me sitting there. It was easier than moving the truck.

It shouldn't be hard to spot me. I was wearing some crazy bright yellow shorts and a bright orange shirt. All the motorists driving by laughing didn't seem to have an issue seeing me. One of the complex parts of dementia is trying to dress yourself. You grab whatever you find and throw it on. I once wore a pair of Kristin's jeans all day without realizing it. I was cussing the whole day because the pockets were tiny and fake. Some days, I'd shave only a part of my face because I would forget to do my entire face. One side would be smooth, and the other would be thick stubble.

I hadn't been sitting out on the porch long when I saw her bright red Chevrolet Aveo inching up Main Street, cruising at a snappy five mph. Mom had bought the most brilliant, bright red one that Chevrolet made. If you don't know what an Aveo looks like, imagine a clown car in a circus driven by my mom, who was legally blind and almost deaf and now in the beginning stages of dementia.

Mom was having trouble telling if my truck was in the yard, so she figured she could get a better look-see if she just stopped, which she did, right on Main Street. The cars that she had pulled out in front of when she left the Dollar General were now all lined up behind her like it was a parade and Mom was the Grand Marshall. Fortunately, because they were being led at a whopping five miles an hour, it was easy for them to stop too.

I lived on the corner of Main St. and Doyle Parker Ave. I had lived in this little town for half my life, and the only time I ever saw a traffic jam was when my mom was leading the pack. Now, the cars at the Doyle

Parker Avenue stop sign, waiting for a bright red Chevy Aveo to pass, were backing up down the street, too. Mom would only turn on her turn signal and waste valuable battery life once she could spot me and knew she would make a right at the intersection. Having been the former Mayor, I knew I had to do something.

That's when I, in my crazy bright, florescent yellow shorts and bright orange shirt, complete with my old work boots I had put on while sitting on the porch to complete my pathic ensemble, leaped off the porch to the front yard and started hollering and waving at her to turn right on to Doyle Parker Ave. and pull up in front of the house.

I thought she had seen me when she made the right turn. Mom did not see me, but everyone involved in this traffic jam sure did. They were all laughing and snickering and remained frozen long after Mom revved her bright red matchbox car back up to five mph and continued to cruise right by the house and out of sight. Mom stared right at me the whole time as I stood in the yard waving and shouting. I knew then it was time for her to quit driving. I turned to the parade of cars still parked on the street, staring at me. I put my hands on the hips of my crazy bright, florescent yellow shorts and yelled, "Okay, the show's over. Move along. They probably still have another rack of these shorts left at Walmart."

I waited what I felt should be a significant amount of time for her to drive the five blocks back home, praying the whole time for the good Lord to give my mom and all the little kids that were about to be released from Bowling Green Elementary for their walk home, traveling mercies. Forty-five minutes passed, and I called. I used the house phone so her caller ID would show her it was me calling from home. Maybe she wouldn't answer like she does when I call from my cell and answer, "Who is this? Where you at?"

Mom answered the phone, "Who is this?"

"It's your son."

"Which one?"

"Randall! Your favorite!"

"Where you at?"

"I'm at my house."

"No, you're not! I was just by there."

"I saw you. I was on the porch, then in the yard, hollering and waving the whole time, but you just drove right by looking at me."

"Well, I didn't see you."

"Everybody else in town did. I don't know how you missed it," I said.

"You going to be home for a while?"

"Yes, I doubt I will go out in public for a week or so now."

"What?"

"Yes, I'll be home. Come on over."

"Okay, I'm coming back over. I got a letter from the State of Florida, and I don't understand it."

"Well, bring it and come on back. I'll be on the porch."

"What?" she asked, not having a clue what I said.

"I'm home!" I yelled a little louder into the phone.

"Okay, I'll be right there."

I returned to the porch and waited for "Flash" to arrive. I contemplated what the letter was about. My oldest son is an attorney, so Mom always thought since he's my son, I'm an attorney by proxy and brought any of her official mail to me to interpret the legal jargon and explain it to her. Usually, this "official" mail was unofficial scam mail wrapped in official-looking wrappers trying to exploit older adults and sell them useless insurance or extended car warranties by scaring them.

Mom's eyesight had worsened, as demonstrated during the drive-by moments earlier. The State of Florida had restricted her from driving at night. She had to take periodic eye tests and submit the reports to the state to ensure it was safe for her to drive during the day. This letter from the State of Florida might be the letter revoking her driver's license. I'd known for a while that day was soon coming. I wasn't looking forward to being the messenger.

Whether it's age or health concerns, it's a terrible feeling to begin to lose one's independence. A person knows that once that day does occur, it won't be long until they can no longer live independently. They become dependent on family members or, worse, the government. They must live with their family or be placed in an adult facility or nursing home. Even before the dungeon days, I had always promised Mom I would never put her into a nursing home. She would mention it to me occasionally. It was her biggest fear. My word and promises are sacred to me. It's always been a part of my Appalachian heritage. But now I was sick and knew it wouldn't be long before I would lose my independence. I also knew her eyesight and hearing were getting worse, and now she was also in the early stages of dementia right along with me, only she was accelerating at a faster pace, or so it seemed.

Mom was still mad at the eye doctor for losing her nighttime driving privileges. I sat there wishing my brother Ron could break the news to tell her. But since I was the oldest, and I did have a son who was an attorney, and my brother only had a black lab named Shadow, I knew by "de facto" the chore fell to me.

After half an hour and one more traffic jam in Bowling Green, Florida, Mom pulled up and parked where I had tried to get her to park on the first drive-by. I decided to remain seated and not show off my outfit again.

As she fought with opening the gate for a little while, she finally walked up to the porch and sat beside me.

"Do you know who I am?" she asked. She had started asking me that every time she came over since she found out I had been diagnosed with early-onset Alzheimer's. Sometimes, she was kidding. Other times, I wasn't so sure.

"Yeah, I think you're Dale Earnhart Jr., the way you have been speeding around the block ahead of the pack. You didn't run over any little kids walking home from school, did you?"

"I haven't seen any little kids."

"That's what I'm afraid of," I said, shaking my head and taking a deep sigh.

"Why don't you kiss my foot! Here! Your son's a lawyer. Tell me what this letter means."

I looked the envelope over, and it was indeed from the State of Florida, but to my relief, not the DMV. Instead, it was from the Division of Retirement. My mom retired from the school system, and her retirement is through the State of Florida. They send out form letters explaining the changes whenever there's a benefit change. As I sat there reading through all the legal mumbo-jumbo, I soon wished it had been from the DMV telling Mom her driving privileges had been revoked. That would have been easier to explain.

In all its infamous wisdom, the State of Florida had decided to send my mom a form letter to inform her that if she's involved in a same-sex marriage, her significant other can now legally be a beneficiary to all of her retirement benefits. I sat there trying not to smile because without looking up, I knew Mom was watching me intently, waiting for me to explain it to her.

"Well, what's it saying?" Mom was not a very patient woman.

I looked up at her and thought, here's an eighty-three-year-old, very hard of hearing, half blind, ultraconservative woman who is far removed and innocent from how the world is becoming. Who, in her sweet Kentucky slang, pronounces lesbian as lisbon, like the capital of Portugal. Now, because of some bureaucrat, who probably got their cushy job because of influence from a rich relative who knew or was related to some-body, four road workers probably lost their positions at the Department of Transportation so that the State could budget that person's salary. Now, to justify losing those four road workers, they had to send a confusing letter to an eighty-three-year-old, hard of hearing, half blind woman who's in the early stages of dementia. A woman who had spent twenty-five years of her life working as a custodian at an elementary school cleaning up little kid's vomit and poop off the bathroom walls so her fifty-six-year-old son with dementia could explain it to her. Life just wasn't fair.

The only thing I had going for me was my best friend, Julie, was a lesbian, and I knew how to pronounce the capital of Portugal, so I knew both sides of the argument and a little geography. Mom sat there waiting for an explanation while I sat there thinking of how to explain the let-ter so that she understood how her same-sex partner was entitled to her retirement benefits. And, what was worse, I had to do this in my loudest voice possible so she could hear me while sitting on my front porch with little school kids now walking by on their way home. Cars are still slowing down, looking at me because I'm still dressed in the brightest, yellowest (if that's a word) shorts that have ever graced the Walmart clothing rack along with my orange shirt and work boots.

"Well, what does it mean? You're son's a lawyer."

"'And my brother has a black Labrador retriever, but that doesn't help me any," I replied.

My first thought was to take the easy way out and tell her that her driver's license was being revoked. While trying to think of the words to explain this to her, I was cussing the State of Florida, the post office, and finally, for whatever reason, Chevrolet for creating the Aveo. Even if I tried to explain it in my best Kentucky hill slang that Mom and I often talk together in, and even if I use Lisbon, the capital of Portugal, for lesbian, I know she's not going to understand it. I took the easy way out and para-phrased the State of Florida verbiage.

"If you were in a same-sex marriage at the beginning of this year, your significant other would be entitled to all your retirement benefits in the event of your untimely death," I blurted out so loud it caused a couple of passing school kids to jump. I had added the "at the event of your untimely death" just because it sounded so legal, and I didn't want to disappoint her as the father of an attorney.

Mom looked at me briefly, taking what I had said all in, and then asked, "What in the shit does that mean?"

"It means if you had a wife at the first of the year and you croaked off, she would be your beneficiary to your retirement."

Without missing a beat, Mom said, "Huh! What in the world would I want a wife for? I don't even want a husband. They don't know what the shit they're talking about!"

I heard a couple of kids snicker as she said that. Mom and I both started laughing. We were both having a good dementia day that day.

Chapter 14

Getting Lost with Dad

Dad and me, ca. 1966

The worst thing about having dementia was when the fog rolled in, and suddenly, I didn't know where I was or where I was going. To me, getting lost is the worst. I've worked most of my life in the woods, wetlands, and swamps of Florida, either surveying or as an environmental water sampler for the phosphate mines. I've roamed unknown hills and hollers of Kentucky, Tennessee, and SW Virginia, doing family history research. I've always been like Daniel Boone, who once said, "I've never been lost, but I was bewildered one time for three days." However, I don't think I've ever been bewildered for more than a few hours, so when the fog would roll into my mind, not knowing where I was at made me terrified. The harder I tried to push the fog back, the thicker it got. The crazy thing about it is I knew this is happening, but I could do nothing to stop it, try as I might.

I had a doctor's appointment about forty-five minutes from home on this particular day. Typically, Kristin would drive me, but on this specific day, she couldn't get off work, so I had to go solo. She had bought me this fancy iPhone, so if I got lost, I could tell it to take me home, and the GPS in it would tell me how to get there.

There were a couple of problems with the phone. One, it had to have a signal for it to work. And two, the most important thing, I had to remember to take it with me. I usually didn't have problems on short trips, especially to familiar locations. I knew how to get to this doctor's office like the back of my hand, so I was sure it would be okay to take a solo trip. Getting there, I was fine, but on the way home, the fog rolled in, and I found myself driving on an unfamiliar street far from home. I didn't know where I was or how to get home.

I could have pulled into someplace and asked someone. However, another side effect of the dementia fog is when it occurs; it brings paranoia and a lack of trust in strangers. I've tried to understand why this happens. It could be a defense mechanism of the brain because there are always monsters hiding in the fog.

I remember riding in a car on the back roads of Kentucky with my mom and younger brother when I was young. A very heavy fog rolled in as we were heading home. It was so thick my mom could hardly see the road. It was dark, and the dirt road had no lines to show where the edge was. As we crept along, I watched the headlight intently reflecting off the fog, knowing monsters were hiding there in the fog to snatch and carry us away. That's the best description or explanation I have for what the paranoia inside the fog feels like.

As my short-term memory worsened, my long-term memory seemed to improve, and I began to use it more. I don't know the medical reason for this. Doctors have different theories. I think it's the Lord's way of replacing something that's been taken away. I began using long-term memories to help trigger a short-term memory in my brain, and when it would work just as quickly as the fog appeared, it would disappear.

I first used this at my home when I had to urinate, and I needed help remembering where the bathroom was in my own house. I remembered back to when Stephanie and I were married, and we brought our firstborn son Eric home from the hospital. I remembered going to the bathroom to get a washcloth to clean him up. Using that memory sixteen years later, I could find the bathroom.

It's my gut feeling from my experience dealing with this; it might be why Alzheimer's patients get that blank look, and everyone thinks they are off in la-la land or have left reality again. They might be trying to recall an old memory to help find their way back out of the fog. This period was one of the saddest points in my life, and I didn't even realize it then. I was too busy trying to function and find my way back.

On this day, while I was driving along lost, a memory of my dad came to me. My dad was a coon hunter. As a kid, I always begged my dad to take me hunting with him. One cold winter night, when I was probably about ten or eleven years old, he came home from work and told me he was going to run a couple of his young hunting dogs, and I could go. Now, my dad was a hunter, not a killer. He seldom killed anything, and if he did, nothing was wasted. It was cleaned and cooked. His greatest pleasure was just in the hunt and hearing the dogs trail. I rushed and got ready to go hunting with my dad before he changed his mind.

We traipsed along in the snow and crossed frozen creeks in the dark, following two young coon dogs. Finally, they hit a trail. Dad and I sat on a log in an open area listening to the dogs howl as they chased the coon. I think this is what Dad enjoyed the most, just sitting there listening to the dogs' trail and talking about coon hunting. He could tell which dog was which by its howl. The blue tick had caught the scent first. He could tell by its first quick yelps. He could tell by listening to the dogs barking and howling which dog was doing what and which dog was which. The blue tick hound was in close pursuit, barking with quick, intermediate yelps. The closer it got to its prey, the faster and higher the pitch of the yelps became. The young redbone hound was bigger and slower but close behind and gave off a long, lonesome howl as it gave chase.

"Shouldn't we go after them?" I asked.

"No, we'll just let 'em run for a while. Let's see what kind of lesson that old coon can teach those young pups. It's like life. Sometimes, young pups think they know everything and run around just doing a bunch of yelping and barking. Then they run into an old, wise boar coon, and he teaches them just how much they really don't know. Their bark will change if they get him treed."

Dad sat on that log and explained that raccoons were some of God's most intelligent creatures. That's why he liked to hunt them. Raccoons are excellent swimmers and will try to head to water and make the dogs lose the scent of the trail. And if they can, and if the raccoon is old and big enough, it will wait for the dog to get in the water, then get on the dog's back and try to drown them. He had brought the young dogs to train that night because it was cold and the shallow creeks were frozen over. This way, Dad told me, if they got on a trail, the raccoon couldn't lose them in the water or, worse, drown the young dogs. He figured if they were chasing an old, wise coon, the coon would probably try doubling back on the dogs to split them up. The coon would then cross its own tracks and pretty soon have the dogs just running around in a circle while it would mosey along on its way. There was no moon as we sat in the crisp night air, but the stars shone brightly. Dad pointed out the Little Dipper and the Big Dipper to me.

"You see the two stars that make up the outside of the Big Dipper? If you draw a straight line from them, it always points to the North Star, that bright one right there, so if you don't know what direction you're heading at night, you can always use that to find your directions," Dad said.

"What if it's cloudy and you can't see the stars?" I asked.

"Always pick a point on the horizon and walk straight towards it if you can. That will keep you from walking in circles like I hear that ole boar coon has got them dogs doing right now," Dad said as he took a long draw on his cigarette. I could see a smile on his lips from the glow of the cigarette fire as it glowed on his face as he listened to the dogs. "Chances are," he continued, "you'll run across something you'll recognize. If you can't see anything on the horizon, find a creek or a branch and follow it downstream. It's going to run into another stream somewhere; just keep walking downstream, and you'll find something you'll recognize, or eventually, it will go under a road somewhere."

"What if none of that works? Then what?" I asked.

"Don't panic, I'll come find you and show you the way home. Listen! That old coon has doubled back just like I figured and got those dogs split. We better go get 'em, or we'll be out here all night while they run in circles. You go that way and get the redbone," he said, pointing towards the west and the long, lonesome howl of the redbone. "I'll get the blue tick, and then meet you back at the house."

"But I'm afraid," I said.

"There's nothing in the dark that's not there in the light. You just have to move slower and look harder. The house is north of us, and right there's the North Star, and if you get lost, remember, don't panic; I'll come find you."

As I drove along lost that day after my doctor's appointment, I thought of what my dad had told me that night. I picked out a tall radio tower off the horizon and drove towards it. I hadn't gone long before I came to an intersection, and just like that, it triggered my memory, and I knew where I was. And, like I did that cold winter night when I caught up with that redbone hound, I followed the North Star and found my way back home. Because of that memory, I once again found my way back home.

Although my dad passed away several years ago, I believe love is eternal; it lives on forever after we're gone, especially the love of a parent for their child. My dad was always an honest man, and when I said that cold winter night while we were coon hunting that I was afraid, he calmed my fears and was true to his words when he told me, "If you get lost, remember, don't panic. I'll come find you and show you the way home." And fifty years later, he came and found me through the memory of what he had taught me.

The next three chapters were written during this period of my life while I journeyed through the fog on days my thoughts were clear enough to write. Chapter 17, "A Farewell to Cats," is the only story that is fictional in this book. I'll explain that story at the beginning of that chapter.

Chapter 15
Wilbur

A dragline mining, similar to the one Wilbur operated

T his story is about a man I knew, named Wilbur, and our unlikely friendship. But before I tell you about that friendship, I need to set a foundation for how the world was then. I grew up before, during, and after desegregation. Until I was grown, I didn't even know what it was. I've lived in the north and the south. I don't know if it was how I was raised or it's just how I am, probably both, but I've paid little attention to all the things that divide us. I've always decided whether I liked or disliked someone by who they were, not what they were. I don't care what race, age, creed, religion, or sexual preference a person is. I've always tried to follow the "golden rule" and treat others how I want to be treated. Don't get me wrong; I'll laugh at and make fun of anybody who's willfully ignorant to amuse myself. But my jokes and pranks are never based on anyone being different from myself.

I started working in the phosphate mines in Florida when I was eighteen. I guess this is when I first started to learn what segregation meant. Looking back, I was in the first wave of a generation entering the workforce after desegregation and the civil rights movement. Before segregation in the Deep South, low-paying, hard-labor, and dangerous-condition jobs were primarily designated for blacks and some poor white trash. After segregation, wealthy corporations started giving more white trash low-paying, hard work, and hazardous-condition jobs to make everyone feel equal and better about themselves. Later, poor blacks and white trash started getting along and uniting against these conditions. To increase profits, some of the owners of large corporations and farms decided to bring in illegal immigrants who would live in worse conditions for half the pay, because it was still better than where they came from, and at least it gave their children hope.

During most of the first half of the 1900s up until the 1950s, miners, and especially Appalachian coal miners, were paid in company script. The script was printed as currency, and every mining company had its own script—sort of monopoly money. The companies would build housing communities near their mines that the miners had to live in. They had large company stores in these communities. The rent for their homes and inflated goods bought at the store could only be paid for with the company script. The companies not only made large profits by paying low wages, they got the wages back from the rent and inflated store prices. This is where the line from an old song, "I owe my soul to the company store," comes from. If a miner lost his life in the mines, his widow and children only had a few days to evacuate the home or marry another miner. There were actual battles fought in southeast Kentucky between the companies' gun thugs and miners trying to organize labor unions. Finally, the miners won out, payment by script was stopped, and pay and conditions improved somewhat.

Folks in the north think this is strictly a southern phenomenon. I worked in a factory in Ohio for a couple of months before returning to Florida. The management style was the same. It's always been a battle between the classes since the beginning of recorded time. The only difference was up north, all these things occurred in the factories. In the south, it happened in the mining and agricultural industries. On a side note, large northern holdings owned or financed most of these southern industries. Okay, I've laid enough foundation, but before I get off my soap box and move this story along, let me say this. We've all been in this mess together for a long time, and until we quit pointing blame at one another and stop believing the lies originating from the only ones that profit from this mess, it will always be. We have to learn to quit trying to fix everyone else and learn to fix ourselves. As I said, we've been in this mess together for a long time, and we'll either improve or destroy it together. Someone said it much better than me; a house divided against itself can't stand. Now, onto the story.

When I began working in the mines, mining, like our society in general, was in a transition between the old and the new. When I first became a miner, mining was at the end of its ancient era, and the new, present-day, "modern" mining era was still a few years away. New technology commonplace today was still in the trial-and-error phase. The EPA and the Clean Water Act had been established but not implemented. Mandatory reclamation of mined lands was in the process of being passed, and the formation of the Mining Safety and Health Administration was still a year away. There was no forty hours of safety training like the new miners get today. You learned from the old miners, or you got hurt or killed.

Except for five years, I spent thirty-eight years working at the mines. When I was about twenty years old, I worked in the pit, and the dragline operator on my shift was an older man named Wilbur. Wilbur didn't like anyone much, and no one much liked old Wilbur.

Everyone on the crew thought it was strange when Wilbur took a liking to me. As I said, Wilbur never acted as if he ever liked anyone. He was old school and especially hated long-haired hippies. Since my wavy strawberry-blonde hair hung to the middle of my back, and everyone said I was crazier than a run-over dog, they thought they'd be fireworks when I was assigned to Wilbur's crew. Most other miners thought the supervisor had put me on the same crew as Wilbur so he would run me off.

My supervisor hated me worst of all. He had a crew cut, was red-faced from all of his drinking, and often bragged he was a grand dragon of some clan somewhere. Before I was put on Wilbur's crew, I worked on the float crew, which was the worst job in the mines at the time and I was the only white person on any of the float crews. This supervisor would sometimes come out in the field where we were working and make me ride around with him. He would promise to get me off the float if I would "rat out" the guys on my crew who may have been drinking or smoking pot. I could smell the alcohol on his breath as we rode in the truck. I wouldn't tell him anything and he would finally get mad and say I was "nothing but a white nigger" and dump me off back with the crew, with the warning he was going to "run me off one day."

I probably would have quit and gone somewhere else, but I've never cottoned to people like him. It brought me so much pleasure seeing how many shades of red I could make his face turn, or how many veins I could make pop out through his crew cut. I've never been one to let someone bully me, so I'd stand up to him. He wasn't used to that. Sometimes, I'd go out of my way to see how mad I could get him. After all, I was nothing but white trash to him, and he wasn't very bright. It became a game to me to see how stupid I could make him look and how often I could do it. The redder his face got, the better I liked it, which is what ended me up on Wilbur's crew.

Wilbur was almost sixty-five years old, ancient to me then, and nearing retirement. He never joked; if he ever spoke to me, he spoke directly, gruffly, and sternly. He hated everything I liked and liked everything I hated. But the two things Wilbur liked were hard work and checkers. For all the things I wasn't, I was good at my job, and no one could outwork me, and I was a pretty good checkers player. We never had any actual words. We just did our jobs and went home with no special bond.

Back then, we worked a seven-day swing shift. A few months after the supervisor put me on Wilbur's crew, we came in on the second shift to relieve the day shift. When we got to the dragline, it was down. The first shift had broken the drag cables and was standing by the big forty-five-cubic-yard bucket when we arrived to relieve them. In the mines, when the dragline is down, the mining stops. The company is losing money, and everybody is in an uproar. Wilbur instantly got pissed when he saw the other crew just standing around waiting for us to relieve them. The crew truck hadn't even stopped when Wilbur started in cussing the first shift dragline operator, who had broken the cables.

"What the hell are you boys standing around for, waiting for us to get here and fix your mess?"

"We can't get the wedge knocked loose. We've been hammering it all day. We're hot and tired and going home. It's your baby now; you rock it." The other operator yells back at Wilbur as he throws his gear in the crew truck.

The wedge is a giant piece of metal that, just like its name, is shaped like a giant wedge. Its purpose is to secure the three-inch-diameter steel cables to the big dragline bucket as it's pulled through the rock by the enormous electric motors inside the dragline housing. In today's technology, they have a large air-driven piston that hammers the wedge loose, but back in those days, we used a twenty-pound sledgehammer to drive it out.

Wilbur looked at me and yelled, "Mink, grab that sledgehammer and show these sons of bitches how to knock a wedge out!"

"Me?" I thought, looking over at the dragline oiler on our crew. "He was twice as big as me and had arms like a football player. Why me?" Later, Wilbur told me the supervisor had instructed him that when there was any sledgehammering to be done, I was to do it. I grabbed the twenty-pound sledgehammer, walked over to the wedge, dug my steel-toed boots into the sand, and thought, "God, I hope I don't break this handle when I miss this wedge." I hated replacing handles, and the rule was if you broke it, you fixed it.

Now, some days it's good to be good, and some days it's good to be lucky, but the best days are when you're both good and lucky. It's always been a source of debate in my mind, thinking back to that day, wondering whether I was good or lucky or the other crew had unknowingly already loosed that wedge. I raised that sledgehammer up in the air and came down with a grunt of everything I had. The head of that twenty-pound sledge-hammer came down and hit that wedge square in the middle, causing that fifty-pound wedge to fly through the air and come to rest right at the edge of Wilbur's feet. Wilbur never flinched or moved. He just looked down at the wedge, looked up at me, who was standing there grinning like a goat eating briars, and gave me an approving nod of his head. That was the first time anyone had ever seen him give an approving nod to anyone before. I only saw him do that one other time after that. It was precisely the outcome Wilbur had hoped for but doubted would happen. Wilbur looked over at the crew we had just relieved, still sitting in the crew truck, staring at the wedge lying on the ground at Wilbur's feet with their mouths wide open.

"Next time you boys can't do your jobs, have 'em call us in early to do it for you. Now get the hell out of our way so we can finish your job and start mining."

That day, I created a bond between Wilbur and me. After he found out I liked to play checkers, that bond blossomed into the most unlikely of friendships I've ever formed with anyone. My work life became a lot easier. Wilbur would bring his boat to work, and we'd go fishing in the phosphate pits after our shift. Other times, when the plant was down, Wilbur would call me over from the pit, where I worked, to the dragline, and we'd pass the time playing checkers and talking. I always thought I was pretty good, but Wilbur was the best checkers player ever. I would think I'd have him backed into a corner, and the next thing I knew, he was jumping all my checkers. Wilbur was always a couple of moves ahead of me. Sometimes, I would take so long to figure out my next move he would nod off, and I'd have to wake him for his move.

During these games, I learned about Wilbur and a lot about life. Although his language at times could be as flowery as mine, he was a profoundly religious man. He always carried his Bible to work with him. Although he could write his name, he'd never learned to read or write. He had been born in Alabama and had to start working as soon as he put it, "could follow a plow behind a mule." Wilbur disliked our supervisor as much as I did. I found out they had started working in the mines years ago together. Wilbur had given him a good old-fashioned ass whooping once after work for how the supervisor talked to him. Wilbur figured he had put me on his crew to get back at him for the "ass whooping." I took great pleasure in that.

Wilbur was the best and smoothest dragline operator I'd ever seen. Like me, he took great pride in the job he did. After we would have a good night of mining, he'd look over at me in the crew truck on our way back out of the mine and say, "Guess we showed those sons of bitches how to mine tonight."

I was the only one who ever knew he couldn't read or write. He'd been in the navy during World War II. After the navy and the war, he started working at the mines. He got married and had a daughter. He had lost his daughter to sickness years before when she was just a child; this brought him tremendous sadness throughout his life.

We sat in the dragline cab on the graveyard shift one night when he related this story. At nearly sixty-five years old, he was still a big, strong man to me. He always spoke in that matter-of-fact, stern tone, but that night, as he sat across from me with the checkerboard spread out on top of a big water cooler between us, I saw a different man. In the dim light of the cab, I saw tears form and fall upon the deep wrinkles on his cheeks. His voice broke, and a soft, tender voice began to speak.

"My little girl was ten years old when she got sick and died. She was my and my wife's only child. I was sitting beside her bed rubbing her hair when she looked at me and said, 'Daddy, please don't let me die; I'll miss you.' That's the last thing she said. She closed her eyes and died. You know how helpless that makes a man feel to watch his daughter die; there's nothing you can do about it. I hated God for a long time after that. I hated everything. I hated my wife. I hated the doctors. I hated myself. It ain't good for a man to hate so much. It rots you out from the insides. I tried to destroy everything I loved, and I almost did."

"What happened?" I asked.

"I don't know. I was sitting one day drinking a bottle of whiskey and started thinking. I thought, you know what, I don't understand why bad things happen, and there's nothing I can do to change the bad things, but one thing I can do, and that was to change me. My daughter left this world, and I can't ever be here with her on this earth again, but I thought, when I leave this world, I can go be where she's at, so I threw that whiskey away, got on my knees asking the good Lord to forgive me. I became a God-fearing man, hoping to be with my little girl again one day. I fail and fall every day, but I do my best every day, and you remember this, son, no matter what anybody thinks of you. You can do as good as the next feller because you can do your best, and that's all anybody can do – their best. As long as I do my best to be my best, I believe that's all the good Lord is asking of me. He did the rest on the cross."

"Is that why you carry that Bible?" I asked, tears dropping off my cheeks now.

"Well, I can't read. It's a reminder that one day I will see my little girl again, and on that day, I won't fail her."

After we had that talk, we didn't play checkers much anymore. Instead, when I had a break in my work, I would go over to the dragline, sit next to Wilbur, and read to him out of his Bible. He seemed to enjoy that more than checkers. When it came time for Wilbur to retire, our crew discussed what to get him as a retirement present. Everyone seemed to be hell-bent on getting him a fishing rod and reel, I finally spoke up and said, "Nope, he's got plenty of fishing rods. I know exactly what he would like." I wouldn't tell anyone, but everyone on our work crew knew Wilbur and I had grown close, so they trusted me, and we all chipped our money. The crew gave me the money with a warning, "he damn well better like it."

At the end of Wilbur's last shift, we gathered outside the mine office with him. I went to my car and returned with two wrapped presents. I gave Wilbur the first one, and he un-wrapped a cassette tape player. Everyone on the crew was giving me the "stank eye" when I gave him his second gift, thinking this gift better be better than the first one. As Wilbur unwrapped the second present, the crew got to see what I saw that night on the dragline when the tears began to flow down Wilbur's cheeks as he saw the entire Holy Bible on cassette tape. Wilbur raised his head and gave me the same approving nod he'd given me the day I'd knocked the wedge out by his feet. That said it all.

I never saw Wilbur again after that day. He was now retired and I quit the mines soon afterwards to sell insurance for a few years before returning to the mines. I found out later that less than a year after his retirement, Wilbur left this world to be with his little daughter again. Me, well, I fully expect to play checkers with Wilbur again one day. I may never beat him, but I'll do my best, because I can do as well as anyone. I can do my best, and that's all Wilbur would expect.

Chapter 16

Just Close Your Eyes and Believe

DK is second from the right in the middle row. I'm back row on the left.

I started coaching when my oldest son played tee ball and coached baseball until my youngest son finished playing AAU ball. I spent over twenty years coaching baseball. I coached in every league from age five to eighteen. I'd sometimes coach two or three leagues in the same year. Through those years, I've coached hundreds of kids at all levels of organized baseball. Some were great, some were good, and some were not so good. I've kept in contact with some of my old players through the years, who are now as old as I was when I coached them. They are paying it forward and coaching teams of their own. I couldn't be more proud of them and pray something I did, as their coach, was a positive influence for them.

But this story is not about any of them. It is about a kid who taught me valuable life lessons, although I was the coach.

Let me explain how this story happened for those who need to become more familiar with Little League Baseball. The league I was coaching in at the time had two leagues for kids in the age group of ten through twelve years old. One was the Minor League, which in Florida played from February through March, and the other was the Major League, which played from April through May. You had twelve players on each team in the majors.

At the end of the Minor League season, the better players were drafted up to the majors to replace the kids lost from the previous year, who had turned thirteen and were ineligible now to play in the majors. If I weren't coaching in minors, where I could get to know the kids I was coaching and playing against, I would have to go scout players at the Minor League games. This particular year, I was only coaching in the majors and had to scout to get an idea of who was ready to draft up to my Major League.

I always had a simple philosophy when I coached. Teach the kids sound fundamentals and discipline, and let them be kids and have fun. I always coached to win, but winning was secondary. Through the years, I won championships and had seasons where we were lucky to win a game. The kids were always the priority. However, I did have rules. I demanded the kids respect the other players, coaches, umpires, and the game itself. I would sit them on the bench if they didn't, whether they were the best or worst players in the league. Unfortunately, not all coaches and parents shared my philosophy.

Most did, and I coached with and against many great coaches and had many great parents throughout my coaching career who shared the same philosophy. But, there are always those few who try to live out their dreams of being professional baseball players through the kids. I learned from experience that most parents and coaches who did this usually weren't very good when they played.

This particular season, I worked a lot of overtime at the mines and couldn't scout the Minor League games much. But, during one of the games I did scout, I saw a kid playing, who I thought would become an outstanding player. I didn't know his name, so I wrote down his number. After the game, I went to the press box to find out the name of this ten-year-old superstar. I gave this player's number to one of my rival coaches, who was keeping the scorebook in the press box at this game. He was one of the few coaches who didn't share my philosophy. He was one of those loud, obnoxious, screaming-and-hollering, constantly-blowing-a-dag-gum-whistle-at-practices type of coach. The kind that wears matching sweats that are a size or two too small, with #1 COACH embroidered on the back of the jersey. One of those types that, if he moved suddenly, his beer belly protrudes and shines from underneath his shirt, which is too small and gives us all a little flash of what could have been but never was, and is never is going to be.

Winning is the only thing that matters because it reflects on him; if he loses, it is never his fault. It's always because an umpire made a bad call or the other team somehow cheated. He's the kind of coach who lives his dreams, which never came true, through his players, usually his own child. Every league has a coach like this, and this guy was ours. I gave him the jersey number of the kid I was scouting, and he gave me this ten-year-old kid's name, or so I thought.

On the evening of the draft, all of us managers gathered at the ball field to pick the players to fill up our rosters for the upcoming Major League season. Once these players were drafted to a team, they remained on that team until they were no longer league-age eligible. If you drafted a ten-year-old, he would be on your team for the next three years. I had won the championship the year before, and I had the last pick in the draft. I was surprised this player was still available when it came to my turn to pick, and all the other teams had passed on him. The rival coach snickered when I announced the kid's name, which he had given me in the press box the week before. I don't know if I wrote down the wrong number or if the rival coach had intentionally given me the wrong name. I suspect the latter, because on the first day of practice, the kid who showed up was not the superstar I had scouted.

After talking to the team and giving them the team rules, I sent all the new players to right field for a pop fly drill to see who could catch. When I hit the pop-up to my first-round draft pick, he came running in as if to catch the ball, but he didn't stop running. He turned and watched the ball sail over his head as he continued to run toward me at home plate with a big smile. It wasn't a regular smile, but a big, cheesy smile from ear to ear like he was having the best time of his life. I looked at one of my assistant coaches with a confused look. He was shaking his head in disbelief and covering his mouth with his hand so I couldn't see him laughing. I knew this was not the player I intended to draft right then.

"Hi Coach!" he exclaimed and stuck his hand out for me to shake, "I would like to introduce myself. My name is Dipish, but my friends call me DK. You can call me DK. Most people think I am Mexican, but I am not. I am from India. I am Hindu. I do not eat meat."

Those were his exact words. I can still hear them today. I shook his hand and said, "Proud to meet you, DK. You first need to throw that plastic glove over there by the bench. You cannot play this game with a plastic glove; you'll get hurt. You can use one of my leather gloves until you can get one. Now get back out in right field, pick up that ball I just hit you, and throw it to second base."

That day, DK became a part of the team and my life for the next three years. His parents owned a local motel, and he had several younger siblings, all little stair steps that looked precisely like miniature versions of him. I found out later that he had never played baseball before that year, and his parents knew nothing about the game. They had bought him a plastic glove for toddlers because they hadn't known any better. His parents were busy running the motel and caring for the rest of his younger siblings, so he didn't have a ride to practice or the games.

For the next three years, I would pick him up and take him home for almost every practice and game. Also, because, as he put it on the first day of practice, he was Hindu and didn't eat meat, for the next three years, I would buy packs of bean burritos. The players all got hot dogs after the games, so I would bring bean burritos to the concession stand to be heated up for DK after our games since he couldn't eat hot dogs.

During ball season, I would go to work at 6:00 a.m. and not get home from practice or games until after 8:00 p.m. It was burdensome to get off work and drive straight to practice. I had to go out of my way to pick him up daily for practice and games, but it became worth it. He was always positive and always smiling. On my roughest days at work, by the time I got to practice with him, he had me smiling. He loved the game and being a part of the team.

DK became the best-loved player on the team by all his teammates and all of us coaches. He was funny, intelligent, and the ultimate team player; he only lacked ability. He improved some over the three years, but never enough to become a starter. He usually always substituted and played the league's mandatory rule of one at-bat and six outs in the field. Unlike most kids and parents, he was never upset or complained about his lack of playing time; he just loved being a part of the team.

Before every game, I would gather the team together outside the dugout, and we would have a prayer. A general prayer for the kids to enjoy themselves, that no one would get injured, and for both teams to be good sports. I knew DK was Hindu and not of the Christian faith. I told him he was welcome to join us in prayer if he wanted but didn't have to if he felt uncomfortable doing so. He promptly told me, "Coach, I'm part of the team. If the team prays, I pray."

When DK wasn't in the game, he sat next to the other coaches or me in the dugout. If he wasn't keeping track of pitch counts or keeping the scorebook, he was eating sunflower seeds and cheering on the team or explaining strategy to us coaches. He had studied and knew the game, so he became a player-coach sort of. He would tell one of his teammates, "Hey, you need to use a lighter bat; you're way behind on your swing" or "Hey Coach, this guy always hits to the left side; we need to shift to the left." He learned the game better than us coaches. He just didn't have the talent to play it very well.

We played a team we should have beaten easily in one game, but they were killing us. We couldn't hit the ball, we couldn't catch the ball, and we couldn't throw the ball. Just mental mistakes one after another. DK was sitting in the dugout watching, getting frustrated, and spitting out sunflower seed shells everywhere. I was standing at the end of the dugout, yelling to the players to get their heads in the game.

"Hey, Coach!" DK called out to me.

"What DK?"

"We're stinking up the place!"

"I know, DK."

"You know why, Coach?"

"Maybe because no one is concentrating, or we just showed up to get a free hot dog after the game today?"

"Nope!" DK said, "This is on you, Coach. You forgot to pray before the game."

I stood there shocked and almost ashamed that a young Hindu kid from a totally different faith had called me out for not praying before the game, but he was right. I immediately called timeout and called the whole team to the dugout. The other team, the umpires, and the stands were all confused. I shouted to the chief umpire that I had forgotten to pray before the game. He took off his face mask and just gave me a dumbfounded look. I told the kids that DK had reminded me we hadn't prayed before the game and to take off their caps and bow their heads. Right there, before God, the opposing team, all the people in the stands, and one dumbfounded-looking umpire, we said our pregame prayer in the fourth inning of the game.

The good Lord must have been listening because it was like someone flipped the light switch on when that team ran back out on that field. We played our best ball and came back and won the game. When I dropped DK off after the game at his parent's motel, he turned and said to me, with that big smile, as he got out of my vehicle, "Don't forget to pray before the games anymore, Coach. It's not fun to stink up the place."

"I won't, DK. Thanks for the reminder."

I only remember certain games through all my years of coaching, but it's never about whether we won or lost. I remember the kids and specific incidents. I once pulled a starting pitcher in the last inning of a game when he was throwing a no-hitter. He disagreed with an umpire's bad call and spewed out an obscenity. He started walking off the mound to the dugout when he realized what he had done and heard me call timeout. He handed me the ball as I met him at the baseline and said, "Sorry, Coach." He knew my rules about respect, even if he was right and the umpire made a terrible call. It was my job as the coach, not my player's, to disrespect the umpire for bad calls, which I did. The umpire approached me while I watched my relief pitcher warm up along the first base line.

"You know, Coach, I was going to toss your pitcher if you hadn't removed him."

"I know that," I said, then added, "But a wink and a nod are all the same to a blind mule. Let's play ball." I turned, walked off, and left the umpire standing there, trying to figure out if I had just complimented or insulted him with an old Kentucky saying.

One year, one of the best players I ever coached was playing shortstop for me when a teammate made an error. He got mad, screamed at his teammate, and slammed his glove on the ground in the middle of the game. I called timeout and put that player on the bench. I told him he would never disrespect the game or his teammates like that again, or he would spend the rest of the season on the bench. I explained when he lost control of his emotions like that, it would cause him to lose control of his discipline to be the best he could be. That kid later became a star athlete throughout high school and got a college degree. Today, he is currently an excellent high school principal and coach. I didn't want to bench him; I knew it would cost us the game. I wanted him to learn the same discipline I had learned years earlier, planting those onions for my dad, but in a less painful way.

I do, however, remember DK's last game. I always had a tradition that in the last game of the season, since it was their final year in the league, the twelve-year-old players got to play the whole game, whether they were starters or not. I had a problem that particular year, though. I had seven twelve-year-olds, meaning two would have to substitute. Every twelve-year-old on the team came to me before the game and volunteered to substitute so DK could play the entire game. In all the years I coached, I never had that happen before or after. That's how much his teammates thought of DK. I discussed it with my assistant coaches, and we decided to rotate our sons during the game and let DK play the whole game.

The game didn't mean a lot as far as the standings went. We would end up in third place in the league, whether we won or lost. The team we were playing, who happened to be coached by the person who had given me DK's name three years earlier before the draft, had more at stake. If they won, his team would finish in a tie for first. If his team lost, they would finish in second place. I knew this coach wanted to win badly and would bring his ace pitcher at us the whole game. I always played to win and I really wanted to beat this coach. But not at the expense of DK not getting to play the entire game, especially when all his teammates had volunteered to substitute so he could play.

We played them close the whole game. We were the home team, and the last inning was like a script written by Hollywood. Our team got a base hit and two walks to load the bases with two out. Then, as fate would have it, it was time for DK to bat. I had a dilemma. We were behind four runs to three, and the opposing ace, who was also the other coach's son, was getting tired and losing control. The other team called timeout, and the coach went out to the mound to scream at his ace pitcher to settle him down.

I looked at DK, still in the on-deck circle, looking back at me, fully expecting me to pinch-hit for him. In three years, DK had never gotten a hit. He had grounded out a few times to the pitcher and been on base by walking or getting hit by a pitch but had never had a base hit. I had a big decision to make. I had several good hitters on the bench, including mine and one of the other coach's son. I could substitute one of them for DK and give us a chance to tie the game or let DK make the last out of the game.

I wanted to beat this arrogant rival coach who was now screaming to his team, "Easy out now, easy out! This kid ain't going to hit nothing."

I called DK over to me. I looked in the dugout at the kids who had volunteered to substitute so DK could play the whole game. They were all waiting to see what I was going to do.

"Here's what I want you to do. This pitcher is tired and wild. We're going to try and get him to throw balls and walk you to first. I want you to get as close as you can to the plate. When the pitcher starts his windup, I want you to square around like you are going to bunt, but before the ball gets there, put the bat back on your shoulders and don't swing. He'll throw the pitch outside or maybe a wild pitch. If the catcher misses the ball, get out of the batter's box because I'm going to send Gordo home."

"Got it, coach," then he repeated back to me everything I had said.

I took my place in the third base coaching box and told my runner at third, Gordo Solis, the fastest player on the team, that he was running on any pitch that got by the catcher. The opposing coach moved his infielders near each side of the pitcher's mound and pulled his outfielders into the infield. This strategy was only used for little kids in Tee-ball and never at this level of play. It was total disrespect toward DK. The other coach knew the few times DK had hit the baseball, it never made it past the pitcher's mound.

I glared over at the opposing coach, who had a little smirk on his fat face. I could feel my blood boil, but I remembered what I had told my star player years before. When you lose control of your emotions, you lose control of your discipline. I leaned over in the third base coach's box, put my hands on my knees, and mumbled a little prayer to myself, "Forgive that other coach over there, Lord, he's an idiot."

The umpire called time in. The pitcher threw the ball, and DK did precisely like I instructed, except he didn't pull the bunt back. The pitch was wide outside, but he poked at it with the bat. "Strike one," the umpire yelled.

The opposing coach laughed and yelled to his pitcher, "Two more pitches. He can't hit. He's scared of you."

I yelled to DK, who looked down at me before the next pitch, "DK, remember what I told you!" On the next pitch, the same thing happened. He poked the bat at a bad pitch. "Strike two!" I called timeout and called DK over to me. He came over and was all nervous. The other coach's comment was getting him rattled. He had two strikes with two outs. One more strike and the game was over.

"Okay, DK, I want you to calm down. Don't worry about him. He coaches that team; I coach you."

"Sure you don't want someone else to bat, coach?"

"Nope, it doesn't matter if we win or lose; the important thing is we don't quit, so here's what I want you to do. I want you to crowd the plate like you have been, but I don't want you to bunt at the ball. When you see the pitch coming, I want you to get out of the way because Gordo is going to steal home on this pitch. When you get in the batter's box, I want you to take a deep breath, close your eyes, and just believe. Got it?"

"Got it, coach, just close my eyes and believe."

When I got back in the coach's box, I gave the steal sign to the runners at first and second base and said to Gordo at third, "Gordo, as soon as the pitcher starts his motion, I want you to go home as hard and as fast as you can."

It wasn't much of a chance, but it was our only chance.

The pitcher lifted his leg, and Gordo took off for home. I turned towards home to watch him run as my other runners took off from first and second. I couldn't believe what I saw. DK was still standing in the batter's box with his eyes closed. Suddenly, as Gordo and the ball neared home plate, DK swung the bat with his eyes still closed. Crack! DK had hit the ball and driven it over the right fielder's head, who was standing on the infield, where his coach had moved him. The ball rolled to the right field fence. Gordo crossed the plate as DK took off for first base, smiling and jumping in the air the whole way. Junior Solis, Gordo's brother, who had been running from second, rounded third and never slowed until he crossed home plate, scoring the winning run.

The right fielder stood in the infield, staring in disbelief at his coach. The ball had landed right where he had been playing before the coach moved him, and he could have made an easy catch for the third out if it hadn't been for his coach's failed strategy. Our dugout erupted and ran to meet DK, hugging and picking him up. It was like a scene from the movie Rudy. We won the game five to four. I looked across the field at the opposing coach and gave him a wink and a nod. It was all the same to a blind mule.

I gave DK the game ball for getting his first-ever hit and winning the game. He was so excited and happy and couldn't wait to get home and tell his parents about the game. When taking him home that night, he smiled all the way home, looking at the ball in his hand, saying, "I just can't believe it, coach, I just can't believe it." He still had his after-game bean burrito in his other hand. He had been too excited to eat it. It was bittersweet, and I hated for the ride to end.

The words that young twelve-year-old said to me when he got out of the truck would profoundly affect me ten years later when I was at the beach in that bungalow with a pistol lying next to me, planning on killing myself. DK got out of the truck, still smiling, holding the game ball in one hand and a bean burrito in the other, and said, "You were right, coach. Sometimes, you have to close your eyes and believe!"

Chapter 17
A Farewell to Cats

Chumpy as I was working on this book

As my dementia began to worsen, and it became more challenging to write and to keep the darkness and depression away. I was writing one day, and the words would slip out of my mind before I could type them. I remember sitting at my laptop one day crying my eyes out because I couldn't remember how to spell "that." T-H-A-T, the simplest of words, and I couldn't remember how to spell the word. The fog was so thick. I just closed the laptop, laid my head on it, and cried. I couldn't even pray and ask for God's help. I don't remember how long I was in this dense fog. For several days, I know. Then, one morning, I woke up, and my mind was crystal clear. It was like the fog had withdrawn, but I did not remember the previous several days. The last thing I remembered was crying on my laptop.

As I drank my coffee that morning, I was scrolling through the internet and ran across a writing contest for the Hemingway Days in Key West, Florida. This was a perfect opportunity for me. Hemingway is my favorite writer. Not so much his stories, although I do love his stories, it's his writing style that's my favorite. Although my writing style differs, I strive to follow his suggestion to write the truest and simplest sentence possible. As you've witnessed by reading this book, I fail miserably at times, but it's always my goal.

If there's one writer I know about, it's Ernest Hemingway. In college, I did my term papers in both English and humanities on the life of Ernest Hemingway. Love him or hate him, he was a fascinating, larger-than-life person. Ole Papa Hemingway and I had a lot in common. Not that I'm larger-than-life, but Hemingway, near the end of his life, had severe dementia to where he was no longer to be able to write. Hemingway lived a life full of depression and suicidal thoughts. He did many stupid things that destroyed his marriages, and he loved many cats—lots of cats, just like me.

I sat at my keyboard on my laptop, trying to think of a story to write for this contest. That's when my oldest and favorite cat, Chumpy, jumped up in my lap as he often did when I was writing. I had bottled-fed him from the time he was a four-day-old kitten. And he and his sisters often knew when the fog was about to roll in and would climb on me, trying to comfort and protect me, or so it seemed. That's when the story hit me— Hemingway's cats.

I once read a book called Hemingway's Cats. The book was all about Hemingway and his love for his cats. The book even named some of his favorite cats. He was as creative and descriptive with his cat's names as I was. I thought about his depression, suicidal tendencies, and battle with dementia. I remembered how depressed he had become at being unable to write anymore, similar to the experience I had just encountered days before. Hemingway had awakened one morning, loaded his shotgun, braced the gun against the doorway, and blown his brains out. He, being the writer he was, had failed to leave a suicide note behind.

As I sat there with Chumpy in my lap thinking of all these things, I began to think, what if he had left a note? What would it have said? One of my favorite books by Papa Hemingway is *A Farewell to Arms*. Then I thought, because of his dementia at the end and his paranoia and mistrust of people, what if he did leave a note, but the suicide note was to his cats, which he loved and trusted? My story for the contest would be a suicide note from Hemingway to his cats, and I would title it "A Farewell to Cats," and I would use the actual names of Hemingway's cats in the story.

There were just a few problems with entering the contest. Because I had been in the fog the previous few days, I had only a few minutes earlier found out about the contest, and the deadline was midnight that day. Also, the entries could be at most five hundred words. When I write, really writing, or cooking with grease, as I like to call it, I can write fast, sometimes fifty to sixty words a minute. My mind, however, goes at one hundred and twenty words a minute, and I can't write a hello in under a thousand words. I decided not to worry about the word count; I would write, then cut and edit the story when finished. Time was a wasting, so I started, and when I finished, it was over twelve hundred words. I started editing and submitted my story online to the contest sponsor, the Hemingway Guild, with fifteen minutes and three words to spare.

The following is the short story I submitted and the only fiction story in this book.

A Farewell to Cats by Randy Mink

My dearest purr factories,

There will be those who question why I leave no explanation. Others will question my selfishness. Unselfishly, I have written volumes of explanations, though I owe no one any. It's to you, my loyal comrades, only you, who have been my substance during the worst times and trusted friends during the best, that anything is owed.

All the things a man cares for, I've enjoyed. Those things are no more; the one thing I've cared for the most has left me with no promise of return. Writing is a lonely life, and I'm as lonely as I've ever been. I should be able to write like I've never before, but the words are no longer mine. They still rush through my mind as untold stories, but now I am unable to pull them from my thoughts before they take their leave. The words appear and dance teasingly before me but change form so rapidly and then disappear through my fingers before I can close my fist. They are like smoke rising from a fire as the storm approaches, twisting and turning and passing invisibly through me, becoming one with the grayness of the clouds and leaving only a stench in my nostrils of my former self.

Every writer knows from the very beginning how the story ends. But only the best and most merciful writers know how to end their story quickly, simply, and with finality. That much is owed to the reader as gratuity for going through the length of the journey with the writer. I've also known the ending to my story from the beginning, and now, I choose my conclusion to be quick, simple, and final as my reward for the journey.

I hope that eternity is kind to us all, dear comrades. You have been my solace and my greatest confidantes. Each of you slipped into the next. Boise to Princessa, Princessa to Friendless, one name into the next, and many more were just plain ole Kitty, but your loyalty was always first-rate. But isn't that immortality, one's life continuing into the next? The same is true with writers as with cats; one story continues into another, and one writer becomes the next.

I hope I have lived this life true enough and learned my lessons well that I might be honored to enter the next as a cat. Perhaps as a polydactyl calico from the royal line of Snow White. Together, we can enjoy our independence sitting on the docks of Key West and awaiting the fishing vessels to return and sharing the scraps of fish heads tossed aside by weathered old men with deep, dark creases carved in the back of their necks through their years at sea, the gratuity for their journey.

The world has now killed me, but it did not break me. May we meet again in a nobler place, my love sponges. I am eternally grateful for your friendship and loyalty.

Forever yours,

Papa

I didn't win the contest. A lady from England did. Hemingway would have liked my story and probably would have thrown up in his mouth a little reading her's. I learned that day. I knew that Hemingway and I had a lot of similarities. We both loved to write simply and honestly and loved cats. I realized that I could still write when I was cooking with grease. I learned that most publishers' and writers' guilds are about popularity and making money, and in a term my momma would use, they don't know beef from bullshit. But the most important thing I learned that day was always to write for the readers and myself and the cats.

This chapter is dedicated to Chumpy. He was my friend, my writing companion, and my confidant. He was with me from the beginning of this book. Chumpy died lying next to me in the bed on October 14, 2023 as I began the last chapter.

Chapter 18

The Corruption
Runs Deep

O n my next visit to the neurologist, I explained that the dementia was getting worse and the journey into the fog was getting
deeper and longer. He changed my prescription to a relatively
new drug called Namzaric. After a few weeks of taking Namzaric, I had a
dramatic improvement. There were still some foggy days but not as deep
or as long in duration. On other days, I felt totally normal. I was able to
concentrate and do more things. I would still write every day. There were
still my daily visits from Mom, who seemed to be getting worse. I was still
on long-term disability and drawing 70% of my regular salary, although a
significant portion now went to insurance premiums. My appeals for social
security disability were still being denied, but Kristin was working as a
registered nurse and making decent money, so we were making it just fine.

Although everything seemed to be going along fine, I always seemed
to be waiting for the other shoe to drop. And it did when I opened the mail
one day and had a letter from my insurance company. They were send-
ing one of their doctors from Miami, Florida for another cognitive test

to evaluate me. At the time, I never thought anything of it. I was used to the testing. The only thing I dreaded was those four-hour cognitive tests, which usually left me mentally drained for several days afterward.

I drove to Lakeland, Florida, met the doctor from Miami, and went through all the mentally draining cognitive tests like I had several times previously. After about five hours of testing and another hour of waiting for the results, the doctor from Miami and the doctor who ran the clinic in Lakeland, Florida, where I went for this testing, and whom I had seen several times before, came into the testing room where I was waiting. The doctor for the insurance company immediately said he had good news, that there was nothing wrong with me and I could return to work. The only thing that puzzled him was my IQ had dropped significantly. I asked what it had fallen to, and he said 60. I laughed in his face.

Now let me ask you readers something. An IQ of 60 is equivalent to a mildly mental disabled third grader. I had written the story in the previous chapter, "A Farewell to Cats," just a few weeks before this test. Do you think a mildly mental disabled third grader could have written that story? I didn't think so, so I laughed in that doctor's face. My IQ before the dementia had been 142, and now he was telling me it was 60. Even with dementia, IQ levels don't drop that significantly.

Then, the other doctor said I had scored extremely high on the hard parts of the test but not so well on the easier portions, which was indicative of me intentionally skewing the test. When she said that, I got mad all over. It's one thing to tell me my IQ had dropped to a mentally disabled third grader's, but it's another to question my integrity, especially after all I had been through in the past year.

I leaned over, and I looked them both square in the eyes. I can get crazy real quick when I get mad like that, and the look on my face must have scared them because they scooted back in their chairs. I'm sure my face was blood red from my blood that was boiling, and I said, "So you're telling me I'm faking this whole time? I've been using the bathroom on myself when I can't remember where the toilet is. You're telling me I'm faking when I can't remember where I'm at, which sends me into a panic, that I sit and cry, or when I can't remember how to spell the simplest of words? And you're sitting there telling me I scored extremely high on the most challenging part of these tests with an IQ of 60? I want copies of all these tests I've taken today!"

"I'm sorry, but we can't give you copies of the tests. Those are property of the insurance company that ordered and paid for the testing," the Miami doctor mumbled.

I regained control of my emotions and said, "I don't think that's all the insurance company paid for. The insurance company has bought off both of you and if the tests are skewed, you two are the ones that skewed them. You both should be ashamed, but I know you're not. The only thing that controls you is greed." With that, I stood up and left the office.

My mind was clear that day and had been since I started taking Namzaric. Except for upsetting my stomach and some bruising when I would bump myself, it was working wonders at keeping the fog at bay. I had no doubts I had scored well that day. When I got home, my low-IQ self drafted three registered letters requesting the results of the tests I had taken. One to the insurance company's doctor, one to the office where I had taken the test, and the last to my insurance company. The only one who responded was the doctor from Miami who had administered the test, and once again, he refused to give me the results.

I filed a HIPAA complaint with the Department of Health and Human Services. I contacted my local state senator and the state representative from my district. I received no response except the standard, "We'll get back to you." It wasn't an election year that year, and all these years later, I'm still waiting for them to get back to me. I contacted a former high school classmate, a state representative in a different district. I had to hand it to her. She did try and was quite sympathetic to my plight. She finally got the insurance company to respond to me. I got a letter with a refund of that month's health insurance premium and a letter stating my health coverage and my long-term disability were terminated. And for an extra kick in the teeth, they would no longer be funding the company they had hired that was pursuing my social security disability claim. I would have to incur all the costs myself.

There I was, for the first time since I was a sophomore in high school. I had no income, and worse, I had no health insurance. The only thing I had going for me was my mind was clear. Fortunately, I had was I had just received my ninety-day supply of Namzaric. Without health insurance, it would now cost me $900 for a month's supply. I couldn't afford that, so I had to work fast. I began taking the Namzaric every other day instead of daily to stretch my supply out. Kristin was making enough money to pay the bills, but it would still be several months before her health insurance open enrollment and she could add me onto her policy. Somehow, my plight wasn't considered a life-changing event and that was the only exception to adding me before open enrollment.

Now, at times, the depression and the darkness would rear their ugly head. I only wrote occasionally. My mind was too cluttered with ideas and busy trying to figure a way out of my situation to concentrate on writing. I think being so busy and the occasional medicinal use of marijuana kept the depression under control when it wanted to envelop me. I began to see my old mental health therapist, who had helped me tremendously back in the dungeon days. I trusted her.

I called my son, the attorney, for advice. Insurance law wasn't his specialty, but he set up an appointment for me with a close associate he trusted. I went to the meeting with my son's associate with all my emails and correspondence, which I had saved. I sat there and explained the whole story from what I could remember. He told me what I already knew.

He explained the lobbyists for the insurance companies and the politicians had passed laws to protect the insurance companies. The lawyer said we could sue the insurance company, but he could almost guarantee that it would be a minimum of five years before we would ever get to court. And when we did, we didn't stand much chance of winning without the PET scan my neurologist had ordered but had been denied repeatedly. Now I knew why the insurance company kept rejecting the test. The attorney said it would all be subjective without hard evidence like the PET scan. The insurance company could afford many more expert witnesses in the field of neurology than we could. Then he suggested the most obvious solution I had been too busy fighting everyone to think about when he said, "Their doctor said you were fine and could go back to work. Unless you have more money than sense, I suggest you return to work. If this happens again, pay for the PET scan yourself, and then we will have something to fight with."

As I drove home, I thought about what he said. I was angry. I was angry at the insurance company and politicians who had betrayed me and everyone like me. I was angry at HIPPA, who refused to force the doctors and insurance companies to give me copies of my test results. I was angry at the doctors that the insurance company had bought off and now con-trolled. I was tired. I had been beaten. The corruption runs deep. I had two options: retire or return to work. It would be almost two years before I could withdraw what remained of my 401K retirement without losing almost half to taxes and early withdrawal penalties. I decided to return to work.

I called Nikki, who had been my HR representative at my old employ-er's. Nikki was the human resource representative I had the most regard or respect for. She was honest and straightforward but always with kindness. You could tell she cared about people. Nikki had helped me immensely from when I first went on short-term until I had gone on long-term. She was unlike any HR person I had ever worked with. She always went above and beyond.

She was the total opposite of the HR representative I had before her. That one woke up every morning and tried to think of a way to fire me. I believe firing employees was almost an orgasmic experience for her.

During the "Me Too" movement, the company instituted a sexual harassment policy, and we had to attend meetings to roll out the new policy. It was mandatory. I had been on vacation during the initial meeting and had to participate in a separate meeting for all the absent employees during the initial rollout.

At the beginning of the meeting, this particular HR representative had tried to embarrass me in front of the class by saying, "We can all thank Randy for having to attend today because he called out during the first meeting, so we had to schedule this meeting." I've never liked people to do that to me, and I especially didn't like her, so I, without thinking, said, "I'm so sorry about that but I didn't call out. I was on vacation during that meeting. But, you must have been in a hurry to see me, which explains why you wore two different shoes that don't match your outfit today." The whole class erupted with laughter. No one liked her. She did a fake laugh, like we were best friends, while giving me a glare from hell. After the meeting, I was verbally reprimanded by her. I responded I thought it was harassment for her to publicly humiliate me in front of the class. Touché. Soon, I was subjected to almost weekly "random" drug screenings over the next year. I'm sure I was randomly tested because of that encounter. I was tested so often that I came to know the gentleman who did the testing at the time by his first name while he stood behind me at the urinal while I peed in the cup. Again, corruption runs deep and in many different ways. I was so happy when Nikki replaced her as my HR representative.

I told Nikki the doctors from our insurance company said I was fine and could return to work. Nikki was happy but said she had never had anyone ever come back to work after going onto long-term disability and would have to research what the company's protocol was for me to return. She said to hang tight, and she would get to work on finding out what I needed to do. After almost a month of doing numerous tests, seeing company doctors and nurses, and jumping through all the hoops, I was cleared to return to work. I had returned to taking the Namzaric daily to keep the fog away but stopped using marijuana for the depression. Anyone returning to work from being off on disability was always drug tested upon their return. Like he had many times before, God always made a way when there seemed to be no way. On July 13, 2016, after fourteen months, the last four without any income or insurance, I returned to work.

Chapter 19

Go Home—Not Die

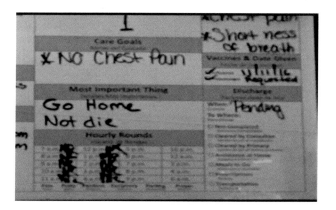

The whiteboard in my hospital room after I left ICU

When I left my job fourteen months earlier, I was an environmental supervisor. Right before I got sick, Rob Larson, the best manager I had ever worked for, was transferred out of the department. I think Rob had ruffled the feathers of our VP, who thought he had a department full of renegades. He, in fact, did, renegades that never had an environmental violation. Renegades that Rob treated like adults and family. He let us do our jobs without micro-managing because that's the way he knew we worked the best. When Rob left our department, the company was in the process of buying out another mining company. After I had been on disability for six months, my position was filled by a younger man from the company that had been bought out. When I came back off disability after fourteen months, instead of returning as a supervisor, I was demoted to a senior environmental technician, the position I had held for many years before my promotion.

Along with the demotion came a very sizeable reduction in my pay and bonus. The pay cut amounted to a fourth of what my salary had been. Still, I was happy to return to work with the old crew. In my mind, I only had to make two more years and could retire. I found when I returned that the whole work atmosphere had changed. The company was in a youth movement, and many of the older folks I had worked with for years had been transferred or offered retirement severance packages. In a short period, the new generation had dismantled the camaraderie and the well-oiled machine Rob had worked hard to assemble. I felt just like Wilbur had when I started working with him many years before. Now, I was just an old man and in the young regime's eyes, no one cared what an old man thought. I kept telling myself two more years and prayed they would offer me a retirement package.

I also prayed the dementia wouldn't return. I knew I was walking a tightrope. Soon after my return, I ran out of all my Namzaric. I had a lot of vacation time built up and figured I would use that on foggy days if I had to. I could have returned to the neurologist for more refills now that I had insurance again. I had burned many bridges with the neurologists and still had a lot of mistrust as far as they were concerned. I decided to take my chances and do without.

Everything was going along well again. I was assigned my old sampling runs, which I knew like the back of my hand. I spent most of my days hiding out and doing water quality sampling in the wetlands, rivers, and creeks of Central Florida. I had always been good at my job, but now I was transitioning into retirement mode. Out of sight, out of mind was my philosophy. I think my new manager and supervisor liked it that way. I had been one of "Rob's boys" and they didn't like dealing with me. I also felt I owed it to Nikki in HR not to create any problems after she had gone out on a limb to put me back to work.

Again, things went smoothly. When I had bad days, I did as I had done in the beginning. I kept it to myself. I decided to take two weeks of vacation—the week before Thanksgiving and the week of Thanksgiving. Kristin took some vacation time and we went to Disney World, where we had season passes. It was her favorite place; mind you, I said her favorite place, not mine. Disney was only a couple of hours away, but we decided to stay several days. We drove home Thursday evening because she had to work that weekend on the cardiac floor at the hospital in Sebring.

My son Kendall came over and we dug up and transplanted a Jasmine bush at the house while Kristin slept during the day for her twelve-hour shift that night. After Kendall left, I showered because I wasn't feeling right. I was having pain in my chest. My left arm felt tingly, and I had a severe cramp in my neck on the left side. I felt lightheaded, but nothing like the dementia had ever caused. I had never had any heart problems before and figured I was just tired from the trip and working in the yard. I took a couple of baby aspirin to be on the safe side.

I showered to see if that would make me feel better but the pain worsened. It felt like my chest would explode. I went into the bedroom, woke Kristin up, and told her how I felt. She sat up in bed, looked at me, and exclaimed, "We've got to go; you're having a heart attack!" We got in the vehicle, and she took off like a bat out of hell. During her last shift at the hospital, she had accidentally left a bottle of nitroglycerin pills in her scrub pocket. She put them in her purse for safekeeping and planned to return them that night. She reached into her bag and started having me put them under my tongue every five minutes.

She bypassed our local hospital and took me to her hospital, where the local hospital would have transported me anyway. What was a regular forty-minute drive took a little over twenty. I told her if I weren't having a heart attack, she would give me one with her driving. She stuck another nitro under my tongue. I asked her if she was trying to overdose me. I got a nurse's glare, and she asked, "Who's the nurse here?" I figured it was best to sit back, watch the fence post fly by, and suck on my nitro.

She wheeled into the ER, and I went to the head of the class. I recall one pill head in the waiting room throwing a fit because they moved me straight into the ER, and she had been waiting long before me to get her pain medication to suffice her addiction. Kristin knew everyone working on me and was rattling off my medical history to them. They were hooking me up to stuff, and I overheard a doctor tell Kristin my EKG was "tombstones," and he had called a STEMI alert. I was having a massive heart attack and was about to die. I still didn't think I was that bad; I was just in a lot of pain. As they rolled me into the cath lab, I called back to Kristin to call my son Eric and have him go to the house and feed the cats and Rudy.

Once in the cath lab, it was like organized chaos. They were hooking me up to all sorts of things. I was getting poked and prodded. I was getting shots of all kinds. Machines were beeping, and alarms were going off. There were many people in there, all doing something. Some were calling off numbers. I still never thought I was in any danger of dying. I remember looking up at the ceiling, thinking I hoped Kristin didn't forget to call Eric to feed the cats and Rudy; it looked like I was going to be late getting home, and suddenly, everything went silent.

I didn't feel my spirit leave my body. I didn't see a bright light. I didn't go through a tunnel. But, I wasn't in the cath lab any longer; I was standing on the bank of a beautiful, crystal-clear river. I felt no pain. If I was the best writer that's ever written, I still couldn't describe the beauty I saw with words. There were colors so brilliant that I'd never seen before. And the music was so peaceful, with notes I'd never heard. It radiated from everywhere: the ground, the rocks, and the sky. And the smells, oh the smells, the only way I can describe the smells is pure. Everything smelled pure. Everything, including me, was enveloped with love so strong it permeated my whole being. It was the *agape* love of God. It was the force that held all that I saw, heard, smelled, and felt together in perfect harmony. I had no idea how I knew all these things, but I just somehow knew.

It was daytime, but the light wasn't blinding or dim. It was like the cool of the evening time. Everything was so clear. I looked up at the sky, but there was no sun. Instantly, the thought came to me that the glory of God was lighting everything. I looked down at my feet, and I was barefooted. Anyone who knows anything about me knows I'm OCD about being bare-footed. I'm never barefooted. The grass was soft but firm all at the same time, and a mist was coming up from the ground. It reminded me of the mist at the grocery store in the produce section that rains down on the produce. It felt so good on my feet.

I stood there taking in all the sights, sounds, smells, and, most of all, the love. I don't know for how long. It seemed like hours, but I had no sense of time. Time no longer existed. I don't know if they had been there the whole time or had suddenly appeared, but I saw two men I instantly rec-ognized. One was my physical father, my dad. The other had always been my spiritual father, my former father-in-law, James Miller, Stephanie's dad. James had been my pastor before, during, and after Stephanie's and my marriage. Even after the divorce, he often would come by and check on me. He was the most faithful and extraordinary man of God I had ever known.

They weren't old anymore. They both looked to be about thirty years old. My dad smiled at me with that big toothy grin he always had. James gave me a smile that said, "See, I told you you'd make it." The *agape* love radiated through me when I looked into their eyes. Without speaking, I knew they were there to escort me across the river to the enormous city rising up behind the mountains behind them.

The mountains reminded me of the high mountains that surround the Cumberland Gap. A giant city rose high behind them. Tall, majestic golden spirals stretched high into the air. Again, I felt no pain. I felt no fear, no worry, no sorrow. All I felt was the love that radiated all through and around me. I never looked behind me, but I could sense nothing was behind me but a giant gulf of nothingness. I knew all I had to do was take one step onto the river, and I could walk on the water to my dad and James, who were waiting to take me to the giant city beyond the mountains. I looked at my feet again with the mist rising about them and started to step onto the water.

As I was about to step, I heard a voice, and I knew it was speaking to me. I recognized the voice. I had heard it before. It wasn't a booming voice but a still, small voice. The only way I know how to describe it is it sounded as if love could speak. I knew instantly it was the voice of the Lord. I still remember exactly what he said.

He said, "I know your journey has been long, and I know how tired you are. You are welcome to enter into your rest but know this: your work is not yet finished. The choice is yours."

I immediately looked across at my dad and James standing on the other side of the river. The river seemed to stop waiting for me to decide. I wanted to run across to my dad and James and never leave this place, but I knew what I had to do. They both looked at me, still smiling, and nodded, affirming I was making the right decision. I smiled and nodded back. I knew what I had to do. I raised my hand in a wave that said I had to leave. In return, they waved back at me, not in a goodbye wave but a "we'll see you again" wave.

"Stay with us, Mr. Mink! Don't go back!" I heard a nurse shouting at me; just as I felt one of the doctors hit me in the chest so hard I felt my sternum crack.

"I'm not going anywhere. Stop hitting me," I replied. In the background, someone said, "He's back. We got him." The alarms started to quiet down. As I lay there, I knew I had been sent back to finish my work and wouldn't die again that night, so I went to sleep and let the doctors and nurses finish whatever they were doing.

When I woke up, I was in ICU, hooked up to all sorts of monitors and IVs. I felt like I'd been beaten with a baseball bat. Kristin was sitting next to the bed.

"Don't you ever do that to me again, Mister! You were clinically dead! You're a miracle!" Kristin said, then started laughing, "I can't believe you're dying as they are wheeling you into the cath lab, and your last words to me are to call Eric to go by the house and feed the cats and Rudy."

I just snickered. I was too out of it from all the medication to carry on a conversation. I woke up a little more clear-headed the next day, and Kristin explained all the medical stuff to me in layman's terms. I had two 100% blockages on my right coronary artery, which they had put stents in. I still had three 99% blockages on my left coronary artery, or the widow-maker as it's called. I would be staying in the ICU over the weekend, and if I were stable and strong enough, they would put three stints in the widow-maker on Monday morning. She also said my brother was bringing my mom to see me because she was about to drive him crazy wanting to see me.

My brother brought my mom to the ICU. Soon after they arrived, the nurse brought me my delicious cardiac patient supper. My mom was all googly-eyeing my food so badly that my brother went to the cafeteria, bought my mom a plate of food, and brought it back to my room. It smelled much better than mine. A side note here: at this point in the visit, my blood pressure, according to all the machines I'm hooked up to, is still doing good, running about 107 over 68.

After my mom finishes her plate, she puts the plastic top back on, takes her plastic knife, decides she's Ringo Starr, and starts beating on the thing as hard as possible. I can hear my little heart monitor thingy beeping faster now, probably to be in the same beat as her drumming. But I doubt that since she had no particular beat to her drumming. It's just random pounding of a plastic knife on a plastic top. And if that's not music enough for me and everyone else on life support in the ICU, she thinks she needs to whistle along with her drumming.

Mom has always whistled this one particular tune as far back as I can remember. What song it's from I know not. In fact, it's not from anything I've ever heard before, so it must be an original composition . . . sort of like her drumming. There is no rhythm, no rhyme, no reason, no tune, and I'm not sure there are even any notes; it's just there. Only now, since she can't hear well, she doesn't think anyone else does either, nor does she care.

When I was little, I heard my dad whistle up horses across a twenty-acre pasture. I've listened to him whistle up coon dogs from the middle of the woods. But never, ever, did I hear my dad whistle as loud as my mom is whistling her little self-composition right now, all the while beating that dang plastic fork on that dang plastic lid, right smack dab in the middle of the cardiac ICU unit.

It's so loud I'm expecting horses to start running down the hall at any moment. I'm picturing poor little dogs all through the city limits of Sebring, Florida, and the outlining areas, turning their heads from side to side, saying, "Make it stop, please make it stop." Whooping cranes migrating south for the winter are refusing to land in the swamps of central Florida. Airliners are being diverted due to sonic interference . . . and my blood pressure is pushing 171 over 98. Kristin was getting nervous because she had pulled some strings with her nurse friends to have that many visitors in my ICU room.

At this point, my life gets saved again for the second time in as many days as my brother tells my mom, "We need to go; you're making alarms go off." Kristin is on the call light to get me a blood pressure shot. I tell my Mom I love her and I will call her when I get out.

I did well over the weekend. Monday morning, I returned to the cath lab to have the other three stents put in the widow-maker. I signed a waiver so they could videotape the procedure. It would be a tricky procedure because two of the stents would have to be done almost simultaneously where the artery branches. The video would be a teaching tool to teach medical students how to do this procedure. I had no fear. I had already died once and been sent back to finish my work. I also had the best cardiac surgeon in the Southeast US, so fear of dying never entered my mind. I just wanted to get out of the ICU and have a decent plate of food like my mom had eaten.

Everything went as planned, and I was taken back to an ICU step-down room. ICU step-down was the department that Kristin worked in, and she knew all the staff on the floor. The doctor had gone up through my femoral artery to do the procedure. I had to lie flat on my back until my blood clotting levels returned to normal from the medication before my nurse could pull the sleeve. A sleeve had been inserted in the artery in my groin to install the stents in my heart. Lying on my back for such an extended period was causing me extreme pain from the herniated disks in my back. I was thrilled when the blood work from the lab came back, and it was okay to pull the sleeve from my groin.

Apparently, the lab got my numbers wrong because when my nurse, one of Kristin's friends she worked with, went to pull the sleeve, I began to bleed out from my femoral artery. My nurse was eight months pregnant and couldn't get enough direct pressure on the artery to stop the bleeding. The charge nurse, another of Kristin's friends, jumped in and started helping my nurse. The pain of four fists pushing into my groin was excruciating. I looked over at Kristin, who was watching them. Through the whole heart attack ordeal, Kristin had kept her nurse's "poker face." Now, I saw panic in her eyes. She jumped up and crammed her fists into my groin with her friend's fists. There I was, totally exposed from the waist down with all my glory hanging out, with three nurses and their fists in my groin. That might be a fantasy for some men, but all I could see was death was trying to get me again. The pain was indescribable, so I did what I'd always done to cope: I started making jokes.

"Well, this is certainly going to make the annual Christmas party uncomfortable for us all," I said.

"Will you shut up with the jokes? Our arms are already exhausted trying to keep you from bleeding to death."

I figured I'd better shut up with six hands in my groin. I turned and stared at the whiteboard on the wall. The nurse had asked when they brought me into that room what my goal was. I said, "Go home and not die." She had written "Go Home—Not Die" on the whiteboard. I concentrated on that until the bleeding stopped, and I was out of the woods again.

When I woke up the next day, my memory was better than ever. I could remember things I had long since forgotten. The cardiac surgeon came in to check on me. He said I was a miracle. I had not suffered any damage to my heart muscle or my brain. If everything still looked good, I could go home the next day.

"Do you think my arteries being clogged could have caused my memory loss and dementia symptoms I had?" I asked.

"Let me put it like this: as clogged as your arteries were, I have no idea how you were even functioning, let alone remembering. You wouldn't have made it if she (nodding towards Kristin) hadn't driven you straight here, giving you the nitroglycerin along the way. You still shouldn't be alive now; I still don't know how you made it."

I knew.

I left the hospital the next day, the day before Thanksgiving. I called my mom as I had promised. Mind you, at the time, I was nowhere near full strength and was on bed rest. It took a lot out of me to talk, let alone yell.

"Hello," Mom said as she answered the phone.

"Hey, I'm home."

"Who is this?" Mom asked, although I had been her son for fifty-seven years with the same voice since puberty.

"Your son!" I yelled as best as I could.

"Who?"

"Randall!" (That's what my mom calls me.)

"He's in the hospital," she replied.

"No, I'm not, I'm home!"

"At your house?"

"Well . . . yes!"

"When did you get home?" Mom asked.

"About noon."

"When? You're mumbling."

I'm thinking to myself, I just had a heart attack for the love of God. The medicine I was on had me very short of breath, but somehow, I was able to scream, "AT NOON TODAY!"

"At two this morning? That's a crazy time to get out of the hospital."

In frustration, I tapped the phone against the side of my head a few times and said, "Yes, at two this morning. It's a new cardiac protocol; they let heart patients out at two in the morning. There's less chance of having a heart attack while it's still dark outside and your heart is still asleep."

"What?"

"I got to go and take some medicine. Love you," I said, not having enough energy to continue the conversation.

"Love you too. I won't come over today and will let you rest."

"Okay, thanks," I said as I hung up the phone.

I immediately turned to Kristin and said, "No need to take my blood pressure. Just give me the pills."

I woke up the next morning on Thanksgiving Day. I felt stronger, but the blood thinners still had me very short of breath. I knew that today my brother, Ron, and sister-in-law, Carla, planned to take my mom some food on Thanksgiving. I also told my kids to bring her some. I knew she would have plenty to eat and be well taken care of. I asked Kristin to hand me my phone. Before I called Mom to wish her a happy Thanksgiving and check on her, I said a little prayer to myself and prayed for strength and so that I wouldn't stroke out on the phone. I said, "Please, Lord, let her hear better today." Sometimes, God's answer to prayer is a no!

"Hello?" Mom said when she answered.

"Happy Thanksgiving!" I said as enthusiastically as I could.

"Happy Thanksgiving! Who is this?" Mom replied.

"Randall! Your son!" I yelled as loudly as possible, knowing the Lord's answer immediately was a big, fat no!

"Ronald and Carla just brought me some food."

"Oh yeah? What did they bring you?" I asked.

"I don't know what it's called."

"What's it got in it?" I asked, trying to figure out what it was.

"It's got some of this and some of that in it, then some kind of meat too," Mom said.

"Well, that narrows it down to almost anything. Have you eaten well today?" I asked, giving up on figuring out what she ate.

"What?"

"Did you eat well today?" I repeated.

"Did I get a fanning?"

"Yes, did someone fan you today?" I asked, tapping the phone to my head again, "I know it's a long-held tradition in our family that we fan each other on Thanksgiving."

"No, nobody's fanning me. Are you crazy? How much medicine do they have you on?"

"Apparently not enough. Put Ronald on the phone!"

"Okay, I'll be over to see you tomorrow. Love you," Mom said.

"Great, I'll be medicated and waiting. Love you too," I said, as Kristin handed me my blood pressure medicine.

I could hear Mom telling my brother as she handed him the phone that she thought I'd lost my mind again. He laughed so hard when he got on the phone he could barely talk, but I surmised that he had brought her some turkey and broccoli casserole. My children had brought her all the other traditional Thanksgiving food and plenty of desserts to last Mom several days. It eased my mind that everyone had taken good care of her on Thanksgiving, and I could now enjoy my cardiac diet meal with a little of this and a little of that, and some kind of meat.

Section Four
Going Home to Finish My Work

My Dad's old house I bought in Kentucky, my home now

Chapter 20

The Promise

Mom and Lady sitting in Mom's favorite swing at the beginning of her dementia

I was off work again on short-term disability until after the first of the New Year. Mom was happy I was home all day again and began her daily afternoon trips by my house to sit on the front porch with me. Mom had stomach issues, so I made an appointment with her doctor. The doctor's office was next door to my home. Mom was now eighty-five years old. I decided to go with her since her hearing was worsening. I also wanted to talk to the doctor about her memory loss, which concerned me more than her hearing.

Mom and I sat down in the waiting room. The doctor had been over-booked as usual, and the waiting room was packed with patients. The office was small and the walls paper thin. I'm not sure how the HIPAA laws apply to walls, but I knew all about the patients in the examination rooms by listening to the doctor and them talking, although they spoke with a normal tone of voice.

I'm on pins and needles the whole time. I never knew what and when Mom was going to say something and say it very loudly with no filter. A few weeks earlier, my brother had taken Mom to church with him and his wife. My brother said everything was going smoothly the whole service until near the end. The preacher was preaching, closing the service, and about to deliver the altar call. Suddenly, without warning and out of nowhere, in that learned-how-to-whisper-in-a-sawmill voice of hers, Mom shouted, "If I were at home, I'd turn him up!" My brother said the laughter from the preacher and congregation pretty much ended that Sunday morning church service.

Mom knew she had a captive audience there in the waiting room. Right on cue, there in the crowded waiting room. She leaned, turned around in her chair, and stuck her face right square in mine. I knew exactly what was coming.

"Do you know who I am?" She asked so loudly everyone in the waiting room jumped and was staring directly at us.

"Yes. You're my crazy mother. My memory is just fine now. You can quit asking me that."

"You're not planning on having another heart attack and dying today, are you?"

"Well, it's not in my plan for today, but neither was the last one," I replied.

"If you do, we're in the doctor's office, and it looks like we'll be here all day," Mom said, her patience growing thin.

The folks in the waiting room all snickered and agreed. The only one who didn't was the receptionist, who slid her glass window closed with a little slam at the end for effect.

"I guess I made her mad!" Mom said and laughed along with everyone else who was running out of patience waiting.

It was hard to guess sometimes why she said the things she said, whether it was to be funny or to get her way, like moving us up to the front of the line at the doctor's office because she had no patience. For whatever reason, it all worked today because about that time, the nurse opened the door and called out, "Mrs. Mink."

I looked over at Mom, who was now looking through a magazine I'd handed her to try and quiet her after her last outburst.

"Mrs. Mink," the nurse called again.

I stood up, motioned for Mom to come on, then looked at the nurse and nodded.

"Where are we going? Home? We've been sitting here forever," Mom shouted.

"No, back here to see the doctor," I shouted back.

"Well, it's about time!" she shouted again, flipping the magazine onto the waiting room table. Everyone snickered again. I know they were all eagerly awaiting to hear the conversation about to come through those paper-thin walls. I wasn't. No one in their wildest imagination was prepared for the discussion about to transpire when we got into the examination room.

The doctor entered the small examination room after all the nurse-related preliminaries. He looked relieved to see me so he could talk to me, and I could translate to my mom through screaming at the top of my voice so he wouldn't have to. I began going through the list of issues Mom had been having in a normal speaking tone.

"Is he talking about me?" Mom yells to the doctor.

The doctor smiles at Mom and nods yes.

"Well, don't listen to nothing he says. He lost his mind years ago. He has to go see a nut doctor," she yells louder. I can hear snickers in the waiting room.

I began to tell the doctor about her memory issues. He thought it had more to do with her age and her hearing. I thought he was full of crap. I knew it was dementia, but I'd already learned from all my dealings with the doctors and neurologists who had misdiagnosed me there was no need to argue with doctors who already had their mind set on something. I told the doctor that she was also having stomach problems.

"Wait right here," the doctor said, got up, and went out the door. In a few moments, he returned, stood at the door, handed me a stool specimen cup, and said, "I'll call all her prescriptions into the pharmacy. Have her put a sample in this cup after her next bowel movement and bring it back to the office." He then turns and leaves for me to explain to Mom.

I stood there holding that stool sample cup and looking at Mom, who was staring at the cup. I wished I had dementia again because maybe one day, I wouldn't remember the conversation I knew was about to transpire. I was sure everyone in the waiting room wouldn't soon forget. I could feel the sudden silence coming from the waiting room. Everyone was sitting with their ears to the walls with bated breath, waiting to hear what was about to be said. I am sure I heard the doctor and nurses have a seat in the waiting room too, so they could also listen.

"What's that for?" Mom asked loudly.

"Oh Lord, help me," I muttered under my breath, then said, "The doctor needs you to put a little bit of stool in this the next time you go to the bathroom," I said to Mom in a lower tone of yelling.

"What?"

"The doctor needs a stool sample," I yelled louder.

"What does that mean?"

"He needs you to put some poop in this cup!" I yelled louder and handed her the cup. Mom couldn't hear, but I could hear everyone listening through the wall laughing now. One man even snorted.

Mom stood there a moment looking at the stool specimen cup, then said, "You're lying. Now tell me the truth. What am I supposed to really do with this?" she said again, getting irritated with me thinking I was teasing her.

"I'm not lying! He wants you to crap in the cup!"

"Ah, shit!" Mom exclaimed.

"Exactly!" I yelled.

That's when the whole waiting room erupted in laughter. I'm positive I heard the doctor and the nurses laughing. When we left the examination room and headed back through the waiting room, everyone had their heads hidden in their hands laughing, or had magazines over their faces, and their bellies were jiggling. The scriptures say a merry heart does good like medicine. I'm sure Mom and I gave a whole waiting room full of people a good dose of medicine that day. To be safe, Mom gave them one more dose right before we walked out the door when she said, "That doctor's crazy if he thinks I can shit in this little cup."

We had driven Mom's little bright red clown car the whole 125 feet to the doctor's office from my house next door because it was hot, and Mom didn't want to walk. The kids were out of school and walking home along Main Street. I was now glad we had driven so the kids didn't have to hear Mom say every ten feet of the journey as she held up the plastic stool sample bottle in from of my face and shouted, "How in the world am I supposed to shit in this little cup?"

This story was the last funny conversation between Mom and me that I ever wrote about. Over the next year, Mom's dementia started to accelerate even faster. There were still amusing stories and conversations. But all the talks and humorous stories had been the real her up to that point. Now, the real person my mom had been started slipping away a little more each day. Before`, she loved my stories and the notoriety they brought her, but now, she wouldn't understand them. The stories and conversations considered funny were now directly due to the disease. Writing them would be like making fun of her, and I loved her too much to do that.

Bowling Green, Florida had a police department full of great and caring officers. I knew many from my days as mayor. On several occasions, I would have two patrol units pull up to my house. Mom would be sitting in the front seat of one car, looking confused. The other vehicle would take me to pick up my mom's car where the officers had found her lost wandering outside her car. Another time, the police found her lost, wandering in the cemetery only a few blocks from her home. Occasionally, I would get a call from a lady at Dollar General who knew both Mom and me and where Mom had always bought her cigarettes every day. Mom would be sitting in her car in the parking lot, not knowing where she was, and I would have to get her and drive her home.

It was time for Mom to stop driving. My brother and I knew stopping Mom from driving would be a sizeable task so we devised a plan. He told Mom that his vehicle needed to go in for repairs and that he needed to use her car for a while until he could fix it. It was a temporary plan, but it would work until we could think of a better one. I snickered as I watched my brother drive away from mom's house in her little red clown car. I figured now we'd find out if it would drive faster than five mph. In the back of my mind, I kept remembering my promise to Mom from the dungeon days that I would never put her in a nursing home. Every day, as mom began to go deeper and deeper into the fog, that promise was always in the back of my mind.

After having my dementia issues for fourteen months and the heart attack, I didn't have the stamina I once had. The old house I'd been trying to repair was falling down faster than I could fix it. After working all day at my job, I would come home, check on Mom, then come back home and work on the house. I had no time to write. Finally, when the water line between the first and second floor of the old house burst and flooded the kitchen I had just remodeled, I told Kristin it was time to move.

We bought a big blue mansion about six miles away. It was 4,300 square feet, completely updated and remodeled with four bedroom rooms and three and a half baths. It came with five wooded acres, a barn, and an in-ground swimming pool. The whole property was fenced. The downstairs had a mother-in-law suite. This area was as large as Mom's entire house. The purchase of this home completely changed my two-year retirement plan because it came with a hefty payment. I knew I'd probably be working until I died, but now my mind was more at ease about the promise. I would have a place for her to live with me.

Kristin and I packed up the thirty-some rescue cats and my old Yorkie, Rudy, who was now almost completely blind, and moved into the big blue mansion. Rudy had been my faithful friend back before Stephanie and I split. Soon, we added seven Pygmy dwarf goats and a dog someone had dumped beside the road, which I named Tip, to join the menagerie of cats in the barn. The goats were a hare-brained plan I came up with for retirement. When I retired, I thought I would sell goat's milk and cheese. It was going to be quite profitable. After I bought the goats, I remembered milking cows as a kid on my grandpa's farm in Kentucky. Milking is an everyday chore. Not only every day but twice a day and one of those two times are early in the morning. I don't do mornings, so the goats became lawnmowers and weed eaters.

Once again, things were going along just fine. I now had a place nice and big enough for family gatherings, and pool, and birthday parties for the kids and grandchildren, which were steadily increasing in number.

All was good except for Mom, who kept declining more and more. It was heartbreaking when she couldn't remember my children's and grandchildren's names. She was getting to the point where she could only remember my brother Ron's and my name. Everyone else was "that boy" or "that girl." I would leave straight from work each day and drive to Mom's to fix her supper. I handled her finances, did her shopping, and took care of what I needed to do for her, then went home and cared for the animals. Every day it was the same routine. My days off were spent doing repairs or running errands. Mom's house was old and getting into a state of disrepair faster than my brother and I could get time to work on it.

The day was rapidly approaching when I would have to move Mom from her home. My brother and I discussed it several times but knew moving Mom would be a death sentence for her. That old, beaten-down house was her home, her place of safety. Without it, she would rather die, I thought. My brother and his wife, Carla, would give me a break from caring for my mom several times a week. Carla, Kristin, and my daughter Julia would go by during the week when they could and clean the house and Mom. I was becoming so exhausted, and in the back of my mind, I kept waiting for another shoe to drop. Soon, it did.

First, Rudy got old and died. It was like losing a best friend. Then, my marriage to Kristin began to fall apart. We soon divorced, but our relationship remained amicable. In fact, we rode to our divorce hearing together, left the courthouse after our divorce was finalized, and spent the day at Disney together wearing the little happy Disney stickers they give you that read, "We are celebrating our divorce." I'd been through too much to be bitter towards anyone anymore. Bitterness is like cancer. It eats you slowly from the inside until it consumes and destroys any goodness left in you.

I had no malice towards Pam and Stephanie and wouldn't have any towards Kristin. I didn't have time anyway. I was so busy I had put both God and my writing on the back burner. My whole life consisted of going to work, taking care of Mom and her place, and then going home to take care of the animals and the big blue mansion, which was even bigger and lonelier now. Kristin was working as an RN hospice case manager. She loved my mom and still stopped by to clean and care for her, often doctoring Mom's mysterious scrapes and cuts she often had. When I would ask how she got them, all Mom would say is, "I don't know." She was never her happy, joking self anymore. She began to look so old, and wouldn't eat. I would often catch her sneaking the food off her plate and giving it to Lady under the table.

Most people didn't understand Kristin and my relationship after the divorce, like no one understood my friendship or relationship with Pam or Stephanie. People like to talk, whisper, and gossip about things that don't concern them. I never cared what the whisperers said. I had no time to deal with the past. I had no time to look towards the future. All I had was the present and Mom. No one understood, and I didn't care. I had no time to deal with the hatred and the pain everyone thinks you should feel after a divorce. That all takes energy and time, and I had neither to spare.

The doctor never did come up with a conclusion about Mom's stomach issues from the stool sample fiasco. It had kept getting worse and I finally had to take Mom to the emergency room, and she was full of gallstones. She was sent to the hospital where I had my heart attack, and they did surgery to remove her gallbladder. After the surgery, we took Mom home; her dementia was worse than ever, and the anesthesia had now brought on hallucinations.

The promise of never putting her in a home always loomed heavily on my mind. I knew the time to move her into the big blue mansion was almost at hand. Every day at work, I was on autopilot. I couldn't concentrate on my work. I was torn, and all I could think about was my promise, and Mom couldn't stay by herself any longer. But I was confused and conflicted, knowing moving her from her home would surely kill her. That place was all the life she had left that was familiar to her. People in the last stages of dementia become very regimented with routine and familiarity. A disturbance in either puts them into a panic. But I had to make a decision.

Mom decided for me. I got a call at work from Ron, who was going to her house. Mom had accidentally set the house on fire. The fire trucks were leaving just as my brother and I arrived, along with my brother's wife, Carla, arrived. Mom had caught the bedroom on fire. She had fallen asleep smoking in bed. Thanks to her neighbor Trina, who had gotten mom out, the house hadn't burned completely down but was now not habitable. Sergeant Eddie Coronado of the Bowling Green Police Department had mom sitting in front of his police cruiser with the air conditioning running to keep her cool. She hadn't been harmed, and Eddie had cared for her like she was his own mother until we got there. I couldn't ever thank him and Trina enough.

As I got Mom out of the police car, she looked at me with the saddest look that broke my heart.

"I really messed up this time. I don't know where Lady is at."

Lady was the dog my brother and Carla had rescued from the animal shelter and given to Mom after Baxter had died. Lady had become her constant companion as Baxter had been.

"You're going to have to stay with me for a while until we can fix your house. We'll find Lady," I said, lying, knowing there would not be any repairs made, but at least it would give her hope until she grew accustomed to living with me. Right on cue, Lady came running across the road and to Mom.

My brother and Carla kept Mom and Lady until I could get contractors to my house to Mom-proof the mother-in-law suite. The blue mansion was two stories and had a long staircase and an in-ground pool. I couldn't take a chance of her falling or drowning. I had to keep her separated from the danger. My kids and I, along with my brother, put up another fence that would contain her and Lady around the area of the house where she would be living. I felt like I was building a prison to control her, which, in reality, I was. I felt so bad and guilty, but all I could think about was my promise.

Mom moved in, and all went as well as possible. I had help from Ron and Carla, my children, and Kristin. I had fixed her a little smoking area on the porch outside her room. I got the swing from her house I had bought her for Mother's Day that she and the Lady liked to sit on outside. I put it inside the fenced-in area under a big, shady oak tree. Not having to go by her old house every day after work was strange. The first day I did. It was just habit. She seemed content except for the barrage of questions she would ask constantly.

Not funny questions like earlier during my interrogations during the dungeon days; these were dementia questions. Where am I at? When am I going home? The hardest ones were when she asked about her sisters or best friend, Maggie. All but one sister were dead. I would tell her they were fine so she wouldn't grieve for them, only to have her mind reset and ask the same question again in a few minutes. There was no sense in telling her she had outlived them and having her grieving every few minutes. Thinking back to how I would ask similar questions when I had been misdiagnosed with dementia helped me deal with her questions tremendously. Mine hadn't been nearly as severe as Mom's was now. I don't know how I could remember my own dementia, but now it gave me an abundance of patience with her I wouldn't have had otherwise.

About a week or so after Mom moved in, I was driving down the long driveway to the house after work. I could see through the fence that Mom and Lady were sitting in the swing. Lady wasn't acting normal. When Lady saw me, she jumped from the swing and started running towards the fence, barking strangely. I made my way through all the locked doors to the swing. I looked at Mom, who was still sitting in the swing. She had the "death stare."

There is a dementia stare where the person stares off into space with a blank look in their eyes. This wasn't a dementia stare; this was the death stare, where no life is left in the eyes. Those who have ever seen it know exactly what I'm talking about. Those that haven't, you will know it when you see it. Hopefully, you won't ever. I've seen it several times, and it still haunts me today. I immediately called 9-1-1. I checked her pulse; she still had one and was still breathing. But there was no response to anything, just a death stare. I shook her, I tapped on her face, I finally stood her up and got her to move. I walked her around, holding her up and talking to her.

Finally, before the paramedics arrived, she came out of it. I mean, completely out of it. She was back almost to her old joking self. The paramedics came, and all her vitals were fine. They wanted to take her to the hospital and get her checked out, but she refused. She acted like her old self from laughing and joking. It was the last time I would ever see her acting her normal self. My brother and Carla came over and stayed awhile. After they left, Mom went to sleep. When she woke up, her dementia was worse than ever. On Mother's Day 2019, everyone gathered at the house; she was coherent but slipping fast.

I called Kristin and told her everything that had happened and wanted to get some nurse advice. At this point, I was totally exhausted. I needed somewhere to turn. I had no more answers. All I had was my promise to Mom from years before. Kristin said she would make some calls the next day and try to get Mom on as a hospice patient and that I needed to get some rest before I became a patient. She volunteered to stay with Mom that night so I could go upstairs and get some rest. She said I would need it soon, along with some professional help for Mom. I agreed.

The next day, Mom was on hospice care at home. Kristin couldn't be her case manager because of the family ties. I asked her to get the best case worker her company had assigned to her case, and she did. They sent Micki. Micki was the perfect fit. She had a warped sense of humor like me and what Mom once had. She was brutally honest and caring. Micki handled Mom like she was her own mother. Micki explained what to expect and what to do when certain things transpired. She went over every detail with a fine toothcomb. Over the next few days, Mom declined rapidly. Lady was always by her side or under the hospital bed hospice had set up at the house.

I called my job and told my supervisor I needed time off to care for my mom. She was dying. Seven years before, when Rob had been my boss, and my dad was dying in Kentucky, he had told me in no uncertain terms to get to Kentucky and take care of my dad for as long as I needed. He told me that family came first. He would take care of everything at work, and he did. I never missed a paycheck. But a new regime ran the show at work now and implemented new policies that benefited a younger generation. The younger employees could now get a month's paid leave if their spouse had a newborn, which was fine; I wish it had been in place when my six children were born. That would have been an extra six months of paid time off. Except for a few people like Nikki, there was no longer loyalty to the older employees. Corporate America had replaced loyalty with greed and selfishness. I was only entitled to forty hours of FLMA to care for a dying parent. I wanted to retire right then and there, but I couldn't, so I took the FLMA.

Over the next few days, I watched Mom become comatose, just like Micki had said would happen. Mom was now receiving around-the-clock hospice care. The caregivers were all so great. As she neared the end, watching the woman I had known all my life as my mother slipping away was gut-wrenching. There were moments of hope when she would be somewhat responsive, followed by hours and days of hopelessness when she would become comatose again. There was guilt that weighed like a millstone around my neck when I wished she would go ahead and pass. I couldn't stand seeing her like that. My promise would soon be fulfilled, but I didn't care any longer about the promise. I just wanted my mom to get better, but I knew that wouldn't happen. Her death stare from the swing haunted me whenever I closed my eyes. Hours felt like days, and days felt like weeks as I watched her lie there.

I remembered Micki and Kristin telling me that hearing was the last of the five senses to leave the body. She could hear us better now, even as unresponsive as she was. No one understood this phenomenon that occurs with the dying. I think it's the Lord's mercy allowing us to tell our loved ones one last time that we love them. I had my kids, my brother, and Carla come over. Everyone sang and talked and laughed like we always had done. We included Mom in the conversations just like she was responsive. I could almost see her foot trying to tap as my son Eric and daughter Julia sang "Shady Grove" to her. I was sure Mom could hear them. I like to think so, anyway. Everyone told her they loved her before they left. Someone said, "If you're ever around the river, drop in." That's what Mom always said to everyone when they left her home back when she was well.

The following morning, I went downstairs to check on Mom. I told the hospice nurse on duty she could take a break, and I'd stay with her for a while. I sat there next to Mom with Lady under her bed. I took her old hand, put it in mine, and stared at it. Her skin was thin and almost transparent. I could see every vein. They were wrinkled and still rough from years of hard work. I looked at mine, and they were starting to look similar. I leaned over and began talking to her against her ear. I thanked her for all the years of love and taking care of me and told her I loved her. Then I said the hardest words, the same words Ron and I had spoken to our dad as he was dying. "It's okay to go. We'll all miss you, but we'll be okay. You taught us well."

I glanced down at Lady looking up at me from under the bed, and it hit me. Before Mom had gotten too bad when she still lived in her home, she asked me to promise to take care of Lady when she died. I never had promised. I leaned back to Mom and said in her ear, "I promise you I'll take care of Lady. I've kept my promise to you. I'll keep the same promise to Lady. It's okay to go." The nurse returned, and I kissed Mom and told her I loved her again. I got up to go into the kitchen to make me some coffee.

As I got to the doorway, the nurse doing her vitals called out to me, "Mr. Mink, she's gone."

I came and sat back down in the chair next to her. She looked at peace. I had all sorts of emotions: sadness, remorse, guilt, grief, the whole gamut that comes with the death of someone you love so dearly. But I also felt relieved that it was over, and she was now crossing over the river I had once stood next to when I had died and returned. I knew she was feeling and seeing all I had felt and more. She was young again. I smiled and thought that she was so stubborn she clung to life until I promised to take care of Lady like I had taken care of her. I looked at Lady with tears and said, "Momma got to go to heaven, and all I got was you." Lady seemed to know already and looked up at me, wagging her little nub of a tail at the new promise I had entered into.

Chapter 21

Going Home

The big blue mansion and Shirley and my table at Marcella's

For over a month after Mom was buried, I dealt with all the usual things. I took care of medical and insurance claims, dealt with social security and state retirement benefits, and sent countless death certificates to everyone to prove Mom was dead. Some wanted the short certificate that didn't show the cause of death, while others wanted the long version that did. I don't know why, in all the money our political leaders like to waste, they don't have some advocate office to assist a person through this process. I know why, but I'll save that for another time.

With my kids' help, Ron and I cleaned Mom's house and sold her home of forty-four years. We threw away stuff, kept stuff, and packed up stuff in totes. Mom had a lot of stuff. What was just stuff to most were trea-sures to Mom. I kept things from the dungeon—the pictures of the owl and Jesus and Baxter's and Lady's dog treat containers filled with colorful empty cigarette lighters. Those were my treasures. Some of the things Mom con-sidered treasures I still have in totes that I haven't dared to sort through.

Finally, everything was finished as I sat outside by the pool behind the big blue mansion in the cool of the evening and began reflecting. Tip and Lady lay beside my feet. Lady had been mourning for Mom, but Tip and she had become the best of friends and Tip had helped ease Lady's grief. I hadn't had time to mourn or grieve. At a time when I should have been exhaling a sigh of relief from all I had been through, I had a great restlessness deep in my spirit I didn't understand. I knew I needed to be somewhere else.

I had begun to hate everything about my job. I hadn't written or talked with God in a long while. I knew the depression and darkness were still waiting in the wings to drag me back to the fog if I dropped my guard. I sat there staring at the pool, knowing there was something I was still supposed to do and that I needed to be somewhere away from the bad memories. I could feel this season of my life was over and a new season was waiting. I just couldn't put my finger on what it was. Suddenly, I heard that still, small, loving voice that had sent me back from heaven years earlier to "finish my work" speak and say, "It's time to go home and finish your work. My gifts and callings are without repentance. You know where your home is and what your work is."

When the Lord speaks to you, there's no confusion or doubt. It doesn't even take much faith to believe. You know that you know. I knew part of my work was to finish all the books and stories I had started over the past thirty-some years. And, the place I wrote best was at my dad's old house in Kentucky. Kentucky was the only place in my life that ever felt like home. I grabbed my cell phone off the table and called my cousin in Arizona, who had bought my dad's old home in Kentucky after he died.

As it always happened, the Lord had gone before me to prepare the way. My cousin Joyce had rented it to someone and was in the process of evicting them because they were months behind on the rent. I offered her the amount the Lord had impressed upon me to offer her, not a cent more or less. Joyce accepted my offer; she was tired of dealing with the renting and repairs. Our attorneys drew up the paperwork, and I withdrew the money from my 401k and mailed her a check. I was going home to Rockcastle County, Kentucky. It was a place I had never lived before, but I knew was home. The restlessness left, and the depression and darkness disappeared into the fog.

I made my first trip with the first load of my belongings to my dad's old home in November 2019. One of my sons, Caleb, came with me on the first trip to help me. It was the first time I'd been inside my dad's old house since he had died seven years previously. I bought it sight unseen.

"Oh my Lord, what have I done?" I asked Caleb. The previous renters had practically destroyed the place.

"Got your work cut out for you, Pops," Caleb said.

Indeed, I did. It still looked somewhat like I remembered, except it looked like my cousin had rented it to a herd of hogs instead of humans. The renters had evidently not paid their electric or water bills either. Since they couldn't flush the toilet, they had used the bathroom in five gallon buckets, put lids on them, and stored them in the garage. Even with holes in the floors and buckets of crap in the garage, it still felt like home. Over the next year, I would make monthly trips from Florida, bringing all my worldly possessions to my new home. My son Jacob and his family came up and helped me build a shed and a cat compound to put all my rescue cats.

Because of COVID-19, I changed my retirement date from April 2020 to June 2020. I remembered leaving my job that last day and driving back down the entrance road. There was no retirement party and no thank you cards or gifts. I had already been locked out of the system that last day and had to get someone to open the door so I could retrieve my personal items.

After thirty-eight years, it seemed like "don't let the door hit you in ass when you leave." I didn't; I just threw my belonging in my personal truck and went back to the house. I was relieved to leave the place I once enjoyed working at, but with the new management, I had begun to hate every day there.

I had no safety net anymore. I had no paycheck and no insurance, and I was a year away from being old enough to draw social security. The freedom was exhilarating and I had no fears. I just remembered what that still, small voice said: "It's time to go home and finish your work. My gifts and callings are without repentance. You know where your home is and what your work is." I had to trust the Lord now, and that's all He ever wanted. I never looked back.

At the end of October, I brought the last load of belongings to Kentucky. My daughter Julia accompanied me. I rented the largest van I could find, took all the rows of seats out, and returned to take her back to Florida and make my last load to Kentucky. I gave all the cats some catnip, and when they were good and stoned, I loaded them into pet carriers I had stacked all through the van. I gave Kristin the keys to the big blue mansion so she could have her dream home again, and I, along with two dogs, and twenty-eight cats heading out from Wauchula, Florida, to Willalla, Kentucky.

As luck would have it, the cat I had positioned right behind my driver's seat did what my Mom couldn't do in the plastic specimen cup at the doctor's office that day. It took the nastiest, smelliest poop inside its cage before I had gotten a mile down the road. I just cracked my window for fresh air. I wasn't stopping until I got to Kentucky, which I did the next day. Except for the twenty-eight cats and two dogs, I was alone for the first time.

That first year, when the weather was good, I worked on the house; when it was bad, I worked on organizing my writings from all the previous years. God had surrounded me with the best neighbors anyone could ask for. Many had known my dad from when he was alive. I was distant cousins and related to half the county where I live. I had no interest in dating or a social life, so I just wrote and worked on my dad's old place, trying to make it mine.

During my first Christmas in Kentucky, my grandchildren bought me a book. It contained questions concerning my life, and I was supposed to answer them and tell them about my life—sort of as a keepsake for them one day when I was gone. I decided I would do them one better, write them a book, and that's when I began this book. As I wrote, it started evolving into the book you are reading today.

The following Christmas, most of my children and all my grandchildren came to visit me. It was so much fun, and I took them to all my exploring sites where my ancestors had settled when they first came to Kentucky. Finally, the holidays were over, and they all had to return to their lives, and I was left to return to this book.

Whether it was because of their visit and now they were gone or because the weather was about to take a turn for the worse, with the cold and gloomy days that Kentucky winter brings to the hills, I started to feel a deep loneliness as I had never felt before. I knew that would open the door to depression and the darkness if I didn't do something. Like I'd done many times before, I tried to outwrite the devil. I couldn't; I developed writer's block.

I had never experienced writer's block. I sometimes write the well dry and have to let it recharge, but I can write anytime and almost anywhere. The weather was getting bad, so I ran to the store while I could. I had plenty of supplies but wanted to get a few extras. Where I live, if I get heavy snow and ice, I cannot go anywhere for a while. Before I could get to a store, the weather turned so bad and so quickly I couldn't drive. I turned around and outran the white-out conditions back to the house. I slid sideways three times before I finally made it home.

I came into the house, and the loneliness was crushing. I bundled up well, went out in the blizzard in my backyard, and recorded one of my stupid weather videos. It wasn't a serious one, just one of my goofs to make me and others laugh and maybe ease the loneliness before the depression and all the darkness could settle in. I returned inside, posted the video to my Facebook page, and tried to write again—still nothing. I couldn't shake the feeling. In desperation, I did the only other thing I knew to do. I bowed my head and prayed.

I said, "Lord, did I misunderstand what you told me? Did you bring me here to die lonely and cold? I feel so alone. I'm all by myself. I feel just like Elijah in the cave. If I heard you right, and this is your will, I'll stay here regardless of how I feel. But, if I didn't hear correctly, and you don't give me a sign, I'm going back to Florida as soon as the weather breaks. My faith is weak, Lord, and I need a sign, and I need it today. I pray in Jesus's name, amen."

I had no sooner got amen out of my mouth and then Bing! My Facebook Messenger went off. I had a message from a Shirley Mullins Gibson, a woman I didn't know. She had seen my goofy video and was laughing and commenting about it. I get messages from people who follow my writings from time to time and I always reply. I usually tell them thank you with a short comment, and typically, that's it. But this felt different. I replied back to her. Then she replied. We ended up texting back and forth for the next four hours. I learned she had moved back to the area about the same time I had moved up here. She had grown up here but moved to Louisiana, where her husband was from. She had just had surgery, chemo, and radiation for breast cancer. During this time, as she battled cancer, her husband left her and they divorced. She moved back to be with her family while she recovered from her treatments. After we finished texting, the loneliness was gone, and I could write, which I did until the wee hours of the morning as it snowed all night. God had given me my sign. I felt again like Elijah when God had sent an angel to feed and minister to him to give him strength for the journey ahead.

As I had figured, I was stranded at home by the snow and ice for several days. So was Shirley, but we talked every day. I still wasn't looking for love or a date, but there was something different about her. We decided to meet and have dinner at a local restaurant that's near both of our homes, called Marcella's, once it was safe for us to drive. I had thought about meeting at my cousin's restaurant, the Limestone Grill, but it was further away and roads still weren't in great shape. Also, I wanted a quick escape in case things didn't go well in person. I'm really not that shallow, but I'd been on blind dates before.

I arrived before she did. A car still with Louisiana plates pulled in. I knew it was her, and I got out of my truck and started walking to her car. The Lord spoke to me in that still, small voice again as I walked towards her and he said, "She's the one. I've gone to a lot of trouble to arrange this. She's still hurting and healing; don't you say anything nor do anything stupid to screw this up." Then I think I heard God chuckle. He knows me better than anyone.

"I'm letting you drive the ship on this one, Lord. I've already shipwrecked too many times," I replied.

When she exited the car, she was exactly as her Facebook pictures depicted her. Her pictures hadn't been photoshopped or filtered. She was just as beautiful as her pictures showed. Her hair was still growing back in from her cancer treatments. It was very short, but I thought it looked beautiful and stylish. We talked until we closed Marcella's down. It was like we had known each other our whole lives. It was like being home. I did like the Lord said and not be my stupid self. We have put him first in our relationship. We have talked or seen each other every day since January 6, 2022. On July 18, 2023, I knelt on one knee and proposed to her inside Marcella's in front of the very table we sat at on that first date. The next time I was in the restaurant, the owner, Marcella Lovell, had "Randy and Shirley" painted on the wall above that table. The Lord was right; she is the one, and one day when he says it's time, we will be wed. They say the fourth time is a charm, or at least I do.

Chapter 22

The Picture Window

The Picture Window at 6520 Hamilton-Mason Rd. taken on May 13, 2023

W riting a closing chapter about your life while you are still alive is hard, but I prefer to do it that way. It's hard to write one if you're dead. My former father-in-law once told me, "I'm not afraid of dying, but if they are gathering up a busload today, someone else is welcome to my seat." I feel the same way. Having died and seen where I'm going, I have no fear of death. What I do fear is not finishing the work I've been called to do to the best of my ability. Whether it's writing this book or the many more I have waiting to be completed.

I didn't mention my children often in this book or go into the divorces. That was intentional. I want to keep their lives private. My children, Randy, Jacob, Caleb, Eric, Kendall, and Julia, have always been my life. They always gave me a purpose for getting up each and every day. My therapist once asked me, if I could change one thing about my life, what would it be? Without hesitation I said, "I would have worked less and given my children more of me instead of things." As far as the ex-wives go, our divorces are no one's business other than ours. We all make mistakes like all people do. It took time, but we stopped blaming, we learned, we started forgiving ourselves and each other, and then we moved on with our individual lives. That's what you're supposed to do, and that's what we did. Now we're friends, and that's all that needs to be written about.

I mentioned earlier in the book that this is not a religious book, and it's not. But it is a book about me and my faith in God. I'm not preachy or judgmental. You can believe however you want. I have enough of a chore to be the best I can be, and most days, I fail miserably. Yet, I strive daily to do what I'm called to do and be what God wants me to be. I'm not accountable to God for anyone else except myself. If that's religious to you, then so be it. What others believe or what others don't believe doesn't affect how I believe.

The bad things I've experienced were caused by my own doing, not the Lord's. But, when I would follow Him, He has always prepared me for the next season of my life from what I learned from the previous season. I don't think it's a coincidence that in the bungalow at the beach, when I was ready to take my life to escape the darkness and depression, a simple prayer my mother taught me as a child popped into my thoughts and became a story that helped me outwrite the devil and find hope again. I don't think it was an accident when I suffered for fourteen months with dementia. It prepared me to be the best caregiver my mom could have ever had when she developed dementia. I understood exactly what she was going through. It gave me a deeper compassion and the strength to keep my promise to her. Nor do I think it was just dumb luck that when I had a massive heart attack, my wife at the time was a cardiac nurse who just happened to have a bottle of nitroglycerin in her bag from her previous shift. I could write many more examples of God's intervention in my life that I haven't included in this book. He always made a way when there didn't seem to be a way.

During Hurricane Charley in August 2004, I was the mayor of the small town of Bowling Green, Florida. Hurricane Charley devastated my town. A reporter from *St. Pete Times* named Lane DeGregory, who later became my friend, asked if she and her cameraman could shadow me for a few days as I worked on recovering my town from the aftermath and do a story. She made me out to be a hero in a story she wrote about me. It got state and national attention. In reality, I had no idea what I was doing. There is no hurricane aftermath training school for mayors. But, I prayed every night after working a twenty-hour day that God would guide me on what to do next and give me the boldness and strength to do it. I wasn't a hero. He just put me in the right place at the right time to be a leader of heroes. The ones I lead were the heroes; I just prayed. It's not mysterious. That's how God works.

I was invited to Tampa to participate in some swanky awards ceremony that I never feel comfortable at. But I was the mayor, so I had to go. I knew it was swanky because they had tablecloths on the table and different spoons, knives, and forks for each entree. I'm more of a roll-of-paper-towels-and-eat-chicken-with-my-hands type of guy. And, of course, as always, I was underdressed for the gala event. The food was delicious and looked expensive, and I wasn't going to waste time trying to figure out which fork or knife to use. I used the same one for everything. I just wipe them off between the different entrees. I'm pretty sure that's why God made fancy cloth napkins and shirttails. They called my name in the middle of a mouth full of prime rib. I had won some prestigious award for my work during the aftermath of Hurricane Charley.

I didn't even know there was an award, let alone that I would win and then have to get up and give a speech with a mouth full of meat. As I got up to give an acceptance speech, I looked up at the podium, and on both sides sat very wealthy people and high-ranking politicians from around the state. I said a little prayer on my way up to the platform. I asked God to rid my mouth of prime rib and fill it with his words because I had no idea what to say. I thanked them for the award and said, "God didn't call me to save the world. He sent his son, Jesus, to do that. All God asks of us to do is be a positive influence in that little part of the world he puts us in. That's all I tried to do with the help of so many others he sent to help me. Thank you." I went and sat back down and finished my prime rib. I was still hungry from not eating well during the hurricane.

I've written all that to preface for the rest of this chapter. Looking back through the years of my life, I can now see how God has always prepared and positioned me for the next chapter or the next season of my life, whether I was aware of it at the time or not. He often used others to do so when I only listened to myself and not him. I'd written this chapter numerous times, but it wasn't right. I would start over and write it again multiple times. It still wasn't right, and I didn't understand why. Usually, the last chapter is the easiest for me. I know where I've been in the story and how I got there, and all I have to do is close it out. I couldn't. Finally, in frustration, I said, "Lord, I don't know how to write it, so you are going to have to write it through me, and I want the last sentence to be your words." I began working on other parts of the book to tighten things up and waited on God to give me this chapter.

In the meantime, I got a text from my lifelong friend Don O'Banion in Ohio. He and his wife, Arlene, are the only two people I had kept in contact with through the years from the high school I attended before moving to Florida at age sixteen. He wanted me to come to the high school reunion they were having in May. I hadn't graduated from there and didn't feel comfortable attending. Then I got a text from the class president, Rick Henry, inviting me to come. He said it didn't matter that I had graduated from school in Florida. I had attended their school for most of my school years, and he would love it if I could attend.

It would be a six-hour round trip, and I'd be gone all day. It's always hard for me to get away for any extended period because of the dogs and all the rescue cats. I have to make a lot of arrangements. I told Shirley about it and all the excuses I had not to attend. Shirley countered every excuse with a good reason to attend. She said she felt like I was supposed to go and she would go with me. I trust Shirley's intuition. She hears from God, too.

We left early on the morning of the Lakota class of 1977 high school reunion in West Chester, Ohio. We had a little time before the reunion, so I drove us to Maud, where I had lived as a child. Everything looked different until I turned off Tylersville Road onto Third Street into the area known as Maud. It was as if it had been frozen in time. I must have been talking a mile a minute and showing Shirley where I was born and where all my aunts, cousins, and Grandma had lived. There were a few updates, but it was mostly as I remembered.

We left Maud and drove the mile and a half to the home where I had been raised on Hamilton-Mason Road. I felt lost on the way; everything looked different. The farmlands and pastures were replaced by huge homes and streets as far as the eye could see until I reached 6520 Hamilton-Mason Road. There it was—my old home, the only house virtually unchanged in the whole area. I drove past slowly, staring at it. I had driven by it a few years earlier after my brother Terry's funeral but hadn't stopped then either.

"Why don't you stop?" Shirley asked as we drove past.

Again, she countered every excuse. She felt like I needed to go back. She said it looked abandoned, and a guy was working out back at the adjoining property. Again, I trusted her intuition. It had gotten me this far.

I turned around at Baxter's old dairy. The old house and a barn were still there and they were the only other things I recognized in the area. We used to buy milk from Baxter's for sixty cents a gallon. I returned to my old driveway, which used to seem so long and turned in. I drove around and past my old house and pulled up to the man working around back at my old neighbor's property. They had long since died. The man's name was Rick. I introduced myself and said that I used to live next door. He told me some of his relations owned my old house, which was scheduled to be demolished. He said the local fire department had been training inside tearing out the ceilings and walls the week before, but I was welcome to go in and look around if I could get inside. He didn't know if they had locked it or not. I was beside myself with excitement. Shirley had been right.

Shirley stayed in the truck as I pulled up to my old house and got out to go inside. I'm unsure if she remained in the truck because her intuition had told her I needed to be by myself for this part of the journey or if she didn't want to be an accomplice in a residential breaking-and-entering crime because locked or not, I was going in. I had been positioned and now I was being drawn in for a purpose. I could feel it.

My hand was shaking as I put it on the doorknob. The last time I was in this house was August 15, 1975, almost forty-eight years previously. It was locked. I was going to have to revert to my old outlaw days and break in, but I was going in. I took my knife out of my pocket and grabbed the doorknob again to jimmy the latch when the door opened without me doing anything.

I took a deep breath and walked inside. A flood of emotion and memories overwhelmed me like a tidal wave. I knew then the Lord had brought me here for a purpose and this last chapter was about to be written. That's why I was there: not for the reunion, but for closure. Closure for the book and me.

My dad's old paneling he had put up fifty years earlier was still in place. The firefighters had torn away the façade the previous owners had put up and exposed the house I remembered. I looked at the wall where the white sheet had been hung as a projection screen. I stood where the kitchen chairs had sat while we watched my dad's home movie extravaganzas. Now, instead of his home movies, the memories from my life were playing instead.

It was the same paneled wall where my brother Terry and I had sat in front of on the couch and divided the Halloween candy—which we had deceitfully gotten by lying—but then felt guilty and sent it all to our brother Gary in Vietnam. God had used those firefighters to bring the home I knew in my memories to life again by removing all the facades. I didn't think that was a coincidence. I thought of how in my life I had put up facades to hide the person I was, or the person I should have been because I feared what others thought. It had taken years of loneliness and pain to strip away my facades. And now, both the facades of wall, and the facades of my life, it was all just trash about my feet. The facades were all gone, but both the wall and I were still standing.

I walked through the kitchen, where we all would sit for supper when we were all together and alive. We talked and laughed while Terry and I fought over the chicken's wishbone. I didn't like the wishbone. I just liked fighting with my brothers. I wished I had the wishbone again, I would wish them all to be there with me alive and a family again. But in my memories, they were. I went into the garage. I looked at the spot where I laid the cat on the freezer to milk it with Dad's nose dropper and then to the spot where my dad and uncles had sat around a washtub waiting for the frozen catfish to resurrect.

I went into the bedroom where all of us boys slept in bunk beds. I could hear my brothers yelling at me for putting my feet under the top bunk from the bottom bunk and pushing up on their mattress to irritate them until Dad or Mom would come in with a belt to calm us down. I remembered where the bed was sitting when my mom woke Ron and me from a sound sleep and whipped us for him running from her when she was going to switch him earlier that day.

I walked back into the living room, and there it was. I had been too blinded by my emotions when I first entered the house to notice. There was the picture window. It was the holy grail of the house. The original wooden trim still surrounded it. The small windows that could be raised on a hot summer day bordered it on each side.

It was the same picture window in front of which the Christmas tree would be placed and decorated every year. The same picture window where I would stand as a kid and watch it snow or rain, or the sun would shine through, and where I watched the robins return without fail in the spring. It was the window where I once stood watching family and friends arrive and then leave again, some never to return.

I stood there staring at my reflection in that picture window. Where a scared young boy had once stood, an old man stared back at me—stripped of his facade by time. I stared deep into his eyes and inched closer to the window, almost trembling. I had to touch it. I took my outstretched fingers of both hands and rubbed them across the glass ever so lightly.

Suddenly, I wasn't alone anymore. On my left was the old man, which was me and whose eyes I had stared into. On my right was the frightened young boy that had once been me. Both stared out the same window but saw from different perspectives. One was trying to see into the future, and the other, looking back at the past.

"What's going to happen to me?" the young boy asked the old man.

"That's going to be up to you, kid. You're going to make it, but it's not going to be easy," the old man replied.

"What's not going to be easy?"

"What do you see when you look out?" the old man asked.

"I see dreams, I see hope," the young boy said.

"That's what everyone wants to see, but what do you really see?"

"The unknown. It scares me," the young boy replied.

"I used to look out this same window, and it scared me too."

"What did you do?"

"I stayed afraid for a long time, and then I had to face it. I found out the unknown is like most bullies. It likes to use fear to keep you from doing what you're supposed to do," the old man said as he looked out across the now busy street and the cluster of progress that used to be woods where his dad had once shown him how to find his way home in the dark.

"The unknown fights you?" the little boy asked, looking perplexed.

"It will fight you every day with fear. You have to fight back, or it'll beat you. You see, kid, everyone is born with their own gifts, talents, and a calling. If the unknown can scare you into not trying to use those gifts and talents, or follow that calling, it wins."

"I don't know how to fight. How do I fight the unknown? I can't see it."

"You don't have to see it. You can feel it. Close your eyes and lean your face to the window," the old man said.

The little boy closed his eyes and leaned his cheek against the window.

"Do you feel the warmth from the sun shining through the window?"

"Yes."

"Your eyes are closed, and you can't see the sun, but you can still feel it. Right?" the old man asked.

"Yes, it's really warm."

"You can't see the sun with your eyes closed but you have faith it's shinning because you can feel the warmth. That's how you fight, with faith. The unknown fights you with your own fear. It wants you to have a fear of failing. A young boy, not much older than you, taught me that when you're afraid you can't do something, you have to close your eyes and believe. You must see with your faith. That's when you can really see."

"Do you ever fail? I hate when people laugh at me when I do."

"Not trying is the only failure. I seldom get things right, but I learn from what I do wrong and try again. As long as you keep trying, you're not failing. And as far as people laughing are concerned, you're going to find that doesn't matter. They only laugh because the unknown made them afraid to try and stole their faith. What else scares you?"

"Monsters!" the little boy said.

"The only monsters that exist are the ones you or the ones you allow someone else to create in your mind. You control the monsters. If you create them, you can destroy them."

"How do you destroy them? I don't understand at all."

"It will take a while, but you'll learn. Truth will destroy the monsters, and then the truth will set you free of them."

The little boy gazed out the window, looking at all the trees in the forest. He sighed deeply and said, "It looks awfully big out there. How will I know my way? How will I not get lost?"

"You'll get lost a lot, even by familiar things. But you have to remember what our father will teach you one day. There's nothing in the darkness that the light won't reveal. And when you can't find your way, don't panic; sometimes you just have to be still and let our father come find you. He'll always show you the way home."

"Will I be rich?" the little boy asked.

The old man stared out the window but looked into his own eyes in his reflection, which led deep within his soul, and snickered at what he saw.

"Riches and gold and the things they can buy you don't mean anything. In the end, they are just numbers that rust and become nothing. But if you allow love to become your gold, then love can always stay, but you must take care of it. And trust me, kid, you'll lose a lot of that type of gold, but you'll find more than you lose. It will take you a long time to learn this, but never take love for granted. Protect and guard it with everything you have. Don't let bitterness, and jealousy, and revenge take it from you. Those are the things that destroy love. Learn to forgive yourself and others when you lose it. If you do that, then you'll find the most powerful love of all. Agape love. That's the God kind of love. Once you find it, embrace it to yourself, care for it every day, and nurture it with all that's within you. And the most important thing is to give more of it away than you get. Agape love will never leave or forsake you and will carry you from this life to the next. You do that, kid, and you'll be the richest person I know."

"I don't think I can remember all that," the little boy said dejectedly.

"You don't have to. It will come to you when the time is right. All you have to do right now is remember what an old man once told me. You can do as well as anyone because you can always do your best, and that's all anyone can do. And when you lose your faith, do what that young boy once told me and just close your eyes and believe. I'll be with you every step of the way. And above all else, remember the prayer momma taught us. It will save our life one day."

With that, the old man, who was me, put his arm around the young boy, who was me, and pulled him close until they both became one with me again. The faith, hope, and love of that innocent child that had once been me, which had been missing for so many years, merged with the old man. I became whole. I knew then I was entering into a new season and a new chapter in my life. I looked out that picture window for the last time before leaving for my class reunion. I thought of my mom and the prayer she had taught my brothers and me, a prayer that many fear because it mentions death. But, because of all I had been through in my life, I no longer feared the monster called death or the unknown. It was a prayer of comfort to me because it had given me life. With tears streaming down my cheeks, I prayed the same prayer I had prayed many years ago in that bungalow on the beach with my pistol lying beside me: "Now I lay me down to sleep. I pray the Lord my soul to keep. If I should die before I wake, I pray the Lord my soul to take. Amen . . . and so be it."

And the Lord said, "Behold, I stand at the door, and knock: if any man hears my voice and opens the door, I will come in to him, and will sup with him, and he with me." Revelation 3:20

The Conclusion

Thank you for taking the time to read my book. I pray it has touched you. I hope it made you laugh and cry, as it made me as I wrote it. If I did, I did my job as a writer. But, most of all, I pray my story gives someone hope. Hope to someone who is at where I have been. Hope to someone currently traveling down the roads I have traveled or those who will. If I made it, you can too; I'm not special. I just had to find the faith in God and myself to never give up.

If you suffer from depression or suicidal thoughts, please get help. Trust me, someone out there loves you and depends upon you. It only takes the first step. Then, it's only one step after the next. The only way things won't change is by not trying to do anything about your situation. So you might fail, no big deal, you try again. Most importantly, stop thinking you can't. An old southern phrase says, "Can't never could do nothing." I was told I could never write a book, and here I am doing it. It took almost sixty-five years, but I never quit or gave up. I just did my best, closed my eyes, and believed. You can do the same.

I shared my soul with you, the reader; if you did enjoy this book, please spread the word. I'm an independent writer without a bunch of money. I don't have a big corporate publisher backing me with a large PR department. It's just you and me. I still believe word of mouth, either spoken or through social media, is the best advertisement.

Please go to my website, www.randymink.com, and sign up to receive notifications when I post information about upcoming books. Sometimes, I post short stories like in this book or previews of chapters to forthcoming books. Or just for the entertainment value of following me to see what kind of foolishness I get into. I'm always into something. Please leave me a comment on the site or at randymink59@yahoo.com. I always try to answer personally; be patient.

I want to say thank you to all my family and friends who stood behind me and believed in me through the years. There are too many to name but you know who you are. Thank you to my granddaughter, Cena Mink, for designing the cover. She nailed it. Thank you to my dear friend Judith George and my cousin Melinda Miller for all the proofreading. You both did a great job of deciphering my jumbled mess. And last but not least, Amy Clouser who hosts my website.

To my dad, Tip Mink, and my mom, Geraldine Mink, who gave me my humor and my heart. To my former father-in-law, Reverend James Miller Sr., who showed and loved me with the love of God despite myself, and to my cat, Chumpy, who always believed in me, I dedicate this book to you all. Not a day goes by that I don't miss and think of your love and what you taught me. We shall all be together again when I step across that river.

Bio

Randy Mink is a southern writer with roots that run deep in the hills and hollers of Appalachian. He grew up listening to his dad, friends, and relatives sitting in the shade on front porches and under the sugar maple trees churning up stories from their lives in the mountains. Randy considered them all master storytellers and credits that experience for his love of storytelling and writing. He says he developed his unique style of writing humorous and heart-tugging stories that bring both laughter and tears by listening to those stories.

Randy moved to Hardee County, Florida, where he won his first writing contest when he was sixteen. He graduated from high school there and, in later years, attended South Florida State College, studying creative writing and English. He says he's been everything from an outlaw in his younger days to a mayor and a jail minister, but most of his life, he was a miner who just wanted to grow up to be a writer.

Through the years, he's always written. In June 2020, he retired after thirty-eight years of working in the phosphate mines of south-central Florida. He loaded up the hundreds of stories he'd written through the years, along with his two dogs and many rescue cats, and moved back to his Appalachian roots to finish his books.